SUFFOLK COAST AND HEATHS WALKS

About the Author

Originally from the West Midlands, Laurence Mitchell has been based in East Anglia for longer than he cares to remember. With a degree in Environmental Science, he worked as a geography teacher for many years before finally reinventing himself as a freelance travel writer and photographer. Never one to follow the crowd, Laurence is especially interested in off-the-beaten-track destinations such as the Balkans, Central Asia and the Caucasus region, and has written guidebooks to Serbia, Belgrade and Kyrgyzstan, as well as *Slow Norfolk & Suffolk* for Bradt Travel Guides. When not venturing off to exotic destinations abroad he likes to explore his own backyard of Norfolk and Suffolk, a region he enjoys just as much as anywhere else.

In addition to writing several guidebooks, Laurence has contributed to a number of travel anthologies and provides regular travel and destination features for magazines including *Hidden Europe*, *Geographical*, *Walk*, *Heritage* and *Discovery Channel Magazine*, in addition to writing world music reviews for *Perceptive Travel* webzine. He is a member of the British Guild of Travel Writers. Find out more at www.laurencemitchell.com.

SUFFOLK COAST AND HEATHS WALKS

THREE LONG-DISTANCE ROUTES IN THE AONB
THE SUFFOLK COAST PATH
THE STOUR AND ORWELL WALK
THE SANDLINGS WALK

by Laurence Mitchell

CICERONE

2 POLICE SQUARE, MILNTHORPE, CUMBRIA LA7 7PY
www.cicerone.co.uk

Printed by KHL Printing, Singapore.

A catalogue record for this book is available from the British Library.
All photographs are by the author unless otherwise stated.

OS Ordnance Survey This product includes mapping data licensed from Ordnance Survey® with the permission of the Controller of Her Majesty's Stationery Office. © Crown copyright 2012. All rights reserved. Licence number PU100012932.

Acknowledgements

I am indebted to Nick Collinson, Nick Marsh and Lynn Allen at the Suffolk Coast and Heaths Unit for their valuable assistance and up-to-date information on the routes described here.

Advice to Readers

While every effort is made by our authors to ensure the accuracy of guidebooks as they go to print, changes can occur during the lifetime of an edition. If we know of any, there will be an Updates tab on this book's page on the Cicerone website (www.cicerone.co.uk), so please check before planning your trip. We also advise that you check information about such things as transport, accommodation and shops locally. Even rights of way can be altered over time. We are always grateful for information about any discrepancies between a guidebook and the facts on the ground, sent by email to info@cicerone.co.uk or by post to Cicerone, 2 Police Square, Milnthorpe LA7 7PY, United Kingdom.

Front cover: Boats along the River Blyth at Southwold (Suffolk Coast Path, Stage 3 and Sandlings Walk, Stage 7)

CONTENTS

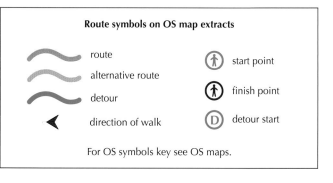

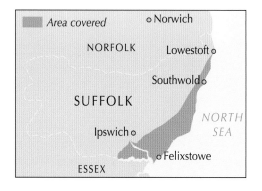

KEY

- Suffolk Coast Path
- Stour & Orwell Walk
- Sandlings Walk

A defensive Martello tower south of Shingle
Street on the Suffolk Coast Path (SCP, Stage 8)

FOREWORD

East Suffolk contains some of the finest and most diverse countryside in lowland Britain. The majority of the coast and immediate hinterland is contained within the Suffolk Coast and Heaths Area of Outstanding Natural Beauty (AONB), a relatively flat, undeveloped landscape of surprising contrasts and distinctive character that borders the southern North Sea.

Walking through the Suffolk Coast and Heaths AONB is the best way to experience the area's wonderful landscape and remarkable stories. There are three long-distance trails within the AONB – the Suffolk Coast Path, the Stour and Orwell Walk, and the Sandlings Walk. Each of these paths has been carefully developed to reveal the most distinctive features of the area, which can be explored in easy stages.

Although this coastal landscape is low-lying, it lacks nothing in drama. Its spectacular views and big skies have made the area famous, but drama of its landscape stems as much from threats the area has faced – natural and man-made – and the way the area has changed in response. Changes here sometimes happen suddenly, such as the infamous 1953 floods, or may take place over a longer period of time, such as the loss of medieval Dunwich, once the most important port in eastern England, which gradually silted up as the sea eroded the coastline.

But change is usually a story that plays out slowly here, and is revealed in the way the AONB's communities have responded to the challenges posed by the sea, the fear of invasion and the unique geology of the area. It can be seen in the many miles of sea and riverwalls, the historic heathland sheep walks, and the lonely Martello towers that punctuate the coastline. The development of the landscape in response to local circumstances is also reflected in the unique natural heritage of the AONB, a landscape that contains some of the most famous nature reserves and rarest wildlife in the UK.

The Suffolk Coast and Heaths AONB challenges many common preconceptions about Britain's coast. While the coastal towns of Aldeburgh and Southwold provide a taste of the traditional British seaside at its best, much of the area confounds conventional thinking about beauty, and challenges notions of a permanent coast 'line'. This is a soft coast, shaped and continually re-formed by the capricious whim of the cold North Sea. It's a sea that is constantly nibbling away at the land, making no distinction between the area's sandy cliffs and small coastal towns, and causing some of the highest rates of erosion in Britain. But it's not all about loss – in other places the sea is building new landscapes and creating some of the most extraordinary coastal features in Britain, such as the shingle spit of Orford Ness.

Behind the coast lies a remarkable area of heathland known as the Sandlings. The Sandlings once covered a vast area of east Suffolk, stretching along the coast from Lowestoft to the edge of Ipswich. The surviving remnants of these heaths are not as wholly natural as they appear, but are a product of the way people have used the land over hundreds, or even thousands, of years – a response to the arid sandy soils of the area. This human influence created an open heathy landscape that became home for plants and animals that would previously have lived only in small woodland clearings. It also established a way of life, based on sheep farming, that whole communities would come to depend on – one that would continue virtually unchanged until swept away in the 20th century by modern agricultural practice.

Another striking feature of the Suffolk coast is its estuaries. All are remarkable, but the two most southerly – the Stour and Orwell – are wetlands of particularly contrasting character. Here, a dramatic tension exists between their beautiful scenery and spectacular wildlife and, in contrast, large-scale human usage – most starkly expressed in the mighty cranes and giant container ships that populate the Port of Felixstowe, one of the largest and busiest ports in Europe.

With miles of footpaths to explore in the AONB, this guidebook opens up to walkers the beauty and history of this unique area. Enjoy your walks!

Nick Collinson
Suffolk Coast and Heaths AONB Manager

A gnarled old tree marks the Freston Wood boundary
(Stour and Orwell Walk, Stage 3)

Former coastguard cottages at Shingle Street (SCP, Stages 7 and 8)

INTRODUCTION

Scots pines at sunset at Bawdsey on the Suffolk Coast Path (SCP, Stage 8)

The sky seems enormous here, especially on a bright, early summer's day, and the sea beyond the shingle almost endless. Apart from the gleeful cries of children playing on the beach, the aural landscape is one of soughing waves and the gentle scrape of stones, a few mewing gulls and the piping of oystercatchers. Less than a mile inland, both scenery and soundscape are markedly different – vast expanses of heather, warbling blackcaps in the bushes, and a skylark clattering on high; the warm air is redolent with the almond scent of yellow gorse that seems to be everywhere. This is the Suffolk coast, and it seems hard

to imagine that somewhere quite so tranquil is just a couple of hours' drive away from London.

The big skies, clean air and wide open scenery of the Suffolk coast has long attracted visitors – holiday makers certainly, but also writers, artists and musicians. The Suffolk coast's association with the creative arts is longstanding, and its attraction is immediately obvious – close enough to the urban centres of southern England for a relatively easy commute, yet with sufficient unspoiled backwater charm for creativity to flourish.

It is not hard to see the appeal – east of the A12, the trunk road that more or less carves off this section of the East Anglian coast, there is a distinct impression that many of the excesses of modern life have passed the region by. The small towns and villages that punctuate the coastline and immediate hinterland are by and large quiet, unspoiled places that, while developed as low-key resorts in recent years, still reflect the maritime heritage for which this coast was famous before coastal erosion took its toll.

The county of Suffolk lies at the heart of East Anglia, in eastern England, sandwiched between the counties of Norfolk to the north, Essex to the south and Cambridgeshire to the west. The county town is Ipswich, by far the biggest urban centre in the county, while other important towns include Bury St Edmunds to the west and Lowestoft to the north. Much of the county is dominated by agriculture, especially arable farming, but the coastal region featured in this book has a wider diversity of scenery – with reedbeds, heath, saltmarsh, shingle beaches, estuaries and even cliffs all contributing to the variety. There is also woodland, both remnants of ancient deciduous forests and large modern plantations. Such a variety of landscapes means a wealth of wildlife habitat, and so it is little wonder that the area is home to many scarce species of bird, plant and insect.

This region can be broadly divided into three types of landscape – coast, estuary and heathland, or Sandlings, as they are locally known – and the

THE AONB

The Suffolk Coast and Heaths AONB was created in March 1970, has a population of roughly 23,500 within its border, and covers 403km² of coastal Suffolk from the Stour estuary at the eastern fringe of Ipswich to Kessingland in the north. This AONB is recognised as one of the most important areas for wildlife in the UK and boasts three National Nature Reserves, the flagship RSPB reserve at Minsmere, several SSSI (Sites of Special Scientific Interest) and wetland sites of national and international importance.

As with any AONB, a balance needs to be struck between the need for conservation of its unique landscape features and its role as an area of both agricultural and recreational use. The Suffolk Coast and Heaths Partnership that manages activities within the AONB is made up of 26 organisations that include local councils and wildlife groups; farming, business, tourism and historical interests; and the Suffolk Coast and Heaths AONB Unit. Based at Melton, just outside Woodbridge, the Unit acts as a champion for the AONB, coordinating the work of the partnership and promoting the area's conservation.

Sandlings heath and conifer plantations at Dunwich Forest (SW, Stage 7)

three long-distance walks described in this guide are each focused on one of these landscape types. All three have plenty to offer visitors in terms of scenery, wildlife and historic interest, and the footpaths, bridleways and quiet lanes found here make for excellent walking.

Almost all the walks in this guide fall within the boundaries of the Suffolk Coast and Heaths Area of Outstanding Natural Beauty (AONB), which stretches south from Kessingland in the north of the county to the Stour estuary in the south. The whole area – both coast and heaths – is now one of 47 Areas of Outstanding Natural Beauty in England, Wales and Northern Ireland, having received AONB status in 1970, a designation that recognises, and protects, the area's unique landscape.

THREE LONG-DISTANCE WALKS

The three long-distance walks described in this guide are the Suffolk Coast Path, the Stour and Orwell Walk and the Sandlings Walk. The first two follow the coast as closely as possible, while the third follows an alternative route through the sandy heaths that lie a little way inland.

The Suffolk Coast Path (sometimes referred to as the Suffolk Coast and Heaths Path) and the Stour and Orwell Walk meet at Landguard Fort, Felixstowe, to provide about 100 miles (160km) of continuous, largely coastal walking – although there are also some inland stretches that are needed to detour around the many estuaries that are a marked feature of this coastline. When combined with these, the Sandlings Walk, which meanders mostly inland for nearly 60

Fingerpost and footpath through reedbeds close to Southwold (SCP, Stage 3)

miles (96km) between Ipswich and Southwold, offers the possibility of a complete circular tour of the Suffolk coastal region for those with sufficient curiosity, time and energy. All three walks have their merits, and all can easily be completed in manageable stages or even cherry-picked as day walks for sections that hold particular appeal.

None of the routes described in this book is especially demanding – all are suitable for newcomers to long-distance walking and all can be done by anyone with a reasonable level of fitness. All the routes are clearly way-marked and involve easy walking on the flat, although some stretches along shingle and sand will inevitably be more tiring, as will muddy paths after wet weather. Facilities are plentiful, and the routes are described in convenient stages with accommodation usually available nearby at the end of the day.

The Suffolk Coast Path
The Suffolk Coast Path stretches along the coast between Lowestoft in the north and Landguard Fort, close to Felixstowe, in the south, a total distance of 55–60 miles (89–97km), depending on whether beach walking or inland options are followed. The path can be walked in either direction, but has been described north to south here in order to link up with a south to north traverse of the Sandlings Walk.

With the exception of the first stage from Lowestoft, this walk lies completely within the Suffolk Coast and Heaths AONB and mostly stays close to the coast. However, coastal erosion in recent years, and the threat of further damage in the future, has necessitated some minor inland diversions in places.

Although the Suffolk Coast Path can be walked at any time of year, the last stage (Stage 8) requires the use of a river ferry between Bawdsey and Felixstowe Ferry, which operates daily only between May and September, and at weekends from Easter weekend to May, and also in October. The optional Orford Loop section on this route (see Stage 6) also makes use of a ferry, between Orford and Butley, which again is seasonal, although this can be avoided by making a longer detour.

The Suffolk Coast Path is described here in eight convenient stages, some of which can be combined, according to fitness levels and time available. The finish point at Landguard Fort, close to Felixstowe, also marks the beginning of the Stour and Orwell Walk, which makes a very natural extension for those wishing to walk further. To walk the complete Suffolk Coast Path route will probably take the average walker between five and seven days – though if you want to build in a rest day somewhere, both Southwold and Aldeburgh, close to Thorpeness, make very pleasant places to take a break.

The Stour and Orwell Walk

The Stour and Orwell Walk continues where the Suffolk Coast Path ends, starting at Landguard Point and threading around the estuaries of the Stour and Orwell rivers to finish at Cattawade, close to the Essex border. This 43-mile (69km) route takes in both the north and south shores of the River Orwell and the north shore of the River Stour. Although much of the way is beside the water, there are inland sections, too, which add to the variety.

In Stage 2, two options are offered for crossing the River Orwell – either a mile-long walk across the busy Orwell Bridge (not to everyone's taste) or the longer 'Ipswich Loop' that passes through central Ipswich, mostly by means of urban parks, and avoids crossing the bridge.

This whole route can be completed over a period of four days, or even three long days for fitter walkers. The route may also be shortened considerably by making use of the seasonal Landguard Fort to Shotley Gate ferry service, which effectively cuts out the Orwell section of the walk (Stages 1–3 and part of Stage 4).

The Sandlings Walk

The third route, the Sandlings Walk (59 miles/94.5km), thoroughly explores the heathland region that lies immediately inland from the Suffolk coast. Beginning at any one of three possible starting points in Ipswich, the route passes through Martlesham Heath

Walkways lead to sailing boats moored on the banks of the River Blyth near Southwold (SCP, Stage 3 and SW, Stage 7)

before following the River Deben estuary up to the pleasant riverside town of Woodbridge. From here it meanders through several tracts of Sandlings Heath and extensive forest plantations before finally arriving at the delightfully old-fashioned resort of Southwold, an excellent place to recuperate. Although almost entirely inland, there is a short coastal section close to Sizewell that is shared with the Suffolk Coast Path. Otherwise, this route offers a different perspective on the hinterland of the Suffolk coast and ideally complements the coastal route.

With the exception of the first stage, between Ipswich and Woodbridge, the route of the Sandlings Walk lies entirely within the confines of the Suffolk Coast and Heaths AONB. To walk the complete length, it is best to allow around five days in total. As well as combining well with the Suffolk Coast Path, the Sandlings Walk could also easily be linked with the first two stages of the Stour and Orwell Walk by taking the Ipswich Loop option of the latter, and then setting out from Ipswich on the first stage of the Sandlings Walk from there to Woodbridge. If this option were chosen, Woodbridge would be ideally placed for a rest day before continuing the Sandlings Walk north. Woodbridge might also be a useful base for completing the next two stages (Stages 2–4) of the Sandlings Walk, as there is little accommodation between Woodbridge and Snape.

In geological terms, this is a relatively young landscape that has some of the youngest rocks in Britain. Underlying the surface geology of the coastal region is chalk, the remnants of a former sea bed from 70–100 million years ago. On top of this is London Clay, laid down around 50 million years ago, and this in turn is overlain in the northern part of the AONB by a cream-coloured sandy limestone, rich in phosphate, called 'crag' that was deposited between 1.6 and 3.5 million years ago. Of the various types of crag found here, Coralline Crag is exclusive to Suffolk.

The coastal landscape seen today is very much influenced by the last ice age – the ice sheets of the last glacial period reached as far south as the Suffolk coast, diverting rivers in their wake and depositing the sands and gravels that characterise the nutrient-poor heaths of the coastal landscape.

HISTORY OF THE LANDSCAPE

The coast

The coast is dominated by two landscape features – shingle beaches and soft, crumbling cliffs. Shingle beaches composed of shelves of small round stones eroded by the action of a dynamic sea are a common feature all the way along this coastline, and even give their name to one settlement south of Aldeburgh – Shingle Street. The cliffs – here composed of

Stepping out on the shingle beach at Dunwich (SCP, Stages 3 and 4)

soft, quickly eroded crag – are seen to best advantage at Dunwich, where the constant and visible crumbling is very much on display.

There were several thriving ports along this coastline in medieval times, mostly notably at Dunwich, one of East Anglia's largest settlements at the time, but also at Southwold and Walberswick. Ongoing coastal erosion in the form of longshore drift meant that the harbours eventually became silted up and, following centuries of booming trade, the maritime business fell into decline, as did the tradition of ship building. (Coastal erosion is still very much a concern, and because of this sections of the Suffolk Coast Path and the Stour and Orwell Walk have been altered and

rerouted considerably in recent years to compensate.)

As a reminder of Britain's maritime tradition, and of the threat of invasion during the period of the Napoleonic Wars, several Martello towers, small defensive forts, can be found along the coast south of Aldeburgh – the northern extremity of a continuous chain of 103 similar structures that stretches all the way down to Sussex.

Some Suffolk coastal towns, such as Southwold and Aldeburgh, underwent a renaissance in the Victorian and Edwardian period, when they were developed as fashionable resorts for wealthy urbanites. In line with this development, the resort village of Thorpeness, north of Aldeburgh, was created more or less from scratch during the Edwardian period. The coastline underwent further changes during World War II, when pill-boxes and gun emplacements were established along the shoreline for defensive purposes, and the curious concrete pagodas at the formerly top-secret base on the Orford Ness peninsula were constructed for weapons testing.

The Sandlings

Inland from the coast, a vast area of heath known locally as the Sandlings once stretched between Ipswich and Lowestoft. Much of this has now gone under the plough or been afforested, but there are still considerable fragments that have been conserved, with their characteristic covering of bell heather and gorse bushes and their rich birdlife.

Settlers first arrived here in the Neolithic period, attracted by light soils that were far easier to work than the heavy clay soils of central Suffolk to the west. Forests were cleared to create land for crops and the grazing of livestock, a process that continued through the Bronze and Iron Age periods. The light, sandy soil of the region ensured that forest was not able to easily re-establish itself, and the now-familiar heaths of the Sandlings developed as a result.

Some idea of the importance and relative prosperity of the Sandlings region in the Anglo-Saxon period may be judged from the treasure found at Sutton Hoo, close to present day Woodbridge. Later, in the 14th and 15th centuries, the wealth created by wool production, resulting from enclosure and grazing of the heaths,

The beach at Pakefield, looking north towards Lowestoft (SCP, Stage 1)

21

financed the building of many fine and notable medieval churches, including those at Blythburgh, Southwold and Kessingland. However, this extensive grazing for wool production caused serious problems of soil infertility in subsequent centuries.

Large areas of heath were enclosed, ploughed and fertilised during the 18th and 19th centuries, and much of the Sandlings region was given over either to game-keeping or arable farming, or afforested with large coniferous plantations.

Forests

All three major forests within the confines of the AONB – Rendlesham, Tunstall and Dunwich – were established by the Forestry Commission in the 1920s on relatively infertile tracts of Sandlings heath. These were all quite badly damaged by the Great Storm of 1987, but widespread clearance and replanting has taken place since. As well as these modern plantations there are also some fragments of ancient woodland with a mix of broad-leaved species.

Estuaries

Estuaries are another notable feature along this stretch of Suffolk coast – with the estuary of the River Blyth separating the former fishing ports of Southwold and Walberswick; the estuary of the River Alde running inland from Aldeburgh to Snape; the estuary of the River Deben at Woodbridge; the larger estuary of the Stour leading

to Ipswich; and, to the south, the Orwell estuary that marks the southern limit of the AONB and, indeed, the county of Suffolk. Although not as busy with maritime trade as they once were, each of these estuaries still has its own character, and all five are popular places for boating.

Since the medieval period, marshland close to the estuaries has been drained and protected by flood walls to create additional farmland. Arable crops tend to predominate, but there has also been a trend towards raising pigs outdoors in fields in recent years, while cattle often graze the wetter meadows.

The low-tide mud flats of the estuaries are important havens for wildlife, especially wildfowl and wading birds, as are the reedbeds and marshes that fringe them. Although valuable for birds and sailors, they are sometimes less convenient for walkers wishing to stay close to the shoreline, as their presence necessitates a certain amount of lengthy detouring away from the coast or the use of some of the ferries that ply the coast.

WILDLIFE AND FLOWERS

Both the coastal strip and the inland Sandlings provide specialised habitat for a range of plants, birds, butterflies and insects – the coast has saltmarsh, shingle ridges, cliffs, reedbeds and grazing marsh; the Sandlings offers heaths, commercial forest and ancient

Nightjar statue near Southwold, one of several nightjar pieces along the Sandlings Walk (SW, Stage 7)

woodland, as well as arable fields and hedgerows.

The Suffolk coast is well known for its bird-watching potential, and the RSPB reserve at Minsmere, with its scrapes, reedbeds, pools and woodland, has long been considered one of the best birding locations in the country. Breeding specialities here include avocets, bitterns and bearded tits, and each year a number of rarities turn up on migration, along with vast numbers of waders and wildfowl. Marsh harriers are relatively easy to spot as they quarter the reedbeds for prey. Lapwings breed on the wet grazing marshes, sand martins nest in holes in seaside cliffs, and little terns and ringed plovers lay their eggs in the open on stretches of shingle. Elsewhere, stonechats and rare

Dartford warblers find a refuge in extensive gorse-covered areas such as Dunwich Heath.

On the shingle beaches, specialist maritime plants such as sea campion, sea holly, sea pea, yellow-horned poppy and sea kale all manage to find a toe-hold, while flowering sea lavender creates a pleasing purple carpet alongside the estuaries. Pockets of broad-leaved woodland with oak, ash and hazel, remnants of the ancient wild wood that once covered the county, provide another haven for wildlife, with shade-loving flowers such as bluebells, wood anemone, red campion and early purple orchid all thriving. In addition, the woodland offers a home to relatively scarce birds including warblers, woodlark, nightingales and nightjars, and woodland

23

butterfly species such as white admiral, purple hairstreak and speckled wood.

The large conifer forests, such as those at Tunstall and Rendlesham, have a more limited flora, but still provide an important habitat for some species of bird and animal, notably muntjac and fallow deer. Since 1987, when the great October storm destroyed large areas of conifer plantation, tree planting has generally been carried out in a more environmentally sensitive manner, with more variety as well as the provision of grassy rides and open glades for wildlife.

Farmland within the AONB is less rich in wildlife than other habitats, but nevertheless provides a home for plant species such as poppy, common mallow and alexanders, as well as bird species including skylark, corn bunting and yellow hammer, and mammals such as brown hare.

The heathland habitat of the Sandlings is home to many birds, as well as interesting butterflies such as grayling and silver-streaked blue, reptiles including the common lizard and adder, and plants such as bell heather, common heather, heath bedstraw, heath speedwell and harebell. One species, the antlion, a scarce and rather strange insect, is found in the UK only in the Sandlings region – most known colonies lie within a restricted area of the Minsmere RSPB reserve. The European antlion (*Euroleon nostras*) is actually the larval stage of a species of lacewing. It earns its name by digging pit traps in

The Royal Hospital School, with its impressively tall clock tower (S&O, Stage 5)

sandy soil and lying in wait at the bottom for other insects, ants or spiders to fall in. It then grabs its prey and sucks the fluid from it through its hollow jaw projections.

CULTURE AND HERITAGE

The slow pace of life and clean air of the Suffolk coast has long attracted writers, artists and musicians. JM Barrie, author of *Peter Pan* (1904), was a regular visitor to Thorpeness, and its artificial boating lake, The Meare, has many landings named after places in the story. The small former fishing village of Walberswick became the adopted home of Philip Wilson Steer and a circle of English Impressionists in the 1890s, and the Scottish architect Charles Rennie Mackintosh came to live and paint watercolours here in 1914. The writer George Orwell, of *Animal Farm* (1945) and *Nineteen Eighty-Four* (1949) fame, once lived and taught in nearby Southwold.

A little further south, Aldeburgh was famously the adopted home of composer Benjamin Britten and his partner Peter Pears; the Aldeburgh Festival, instigated by Britten in 1948, remains an important event in the cultural calendar. The Suffolk coast informed much of Britten's work – the opera *Peter Grimes*, with its libretto based upon the poems of the Aldeburgh poet George Crabbe, tells the tragic tale of a local fisherman. 'The Scallop', a large steel sculpture in the form of a shell by the Suffolk artist Maggi Hambling, stands on the beach at Aldeburgh and bears a quote from *Peter Grimes* – 'I hear those voices that will not be drowned' – as a tribute to the composer. The sculpture is, however, disliked by many residents and has suffered from frequent graffiti attacks.

Woodbridge, too, has had artistic connections – Edward Fitzgerald, the eccentric translator of Omar Khayyam, befriended local fishermen here and spent much of his spare time on sailing expeditions in the area. Arthur Ransome, of *Swallows and Amazons* fame, was another famous author who came to live locally, at Broke Hall Farm at Levington on the Orwell estuary, where he wrote *We Didn't Mean to Go to Sea*, about an accidental sailing voyage on the North Sea.

GETTING THERE AND BACK

The main towns at the start and end points of these walks – Lowestoft, Ipswich, Woodbridge and Felixstowe – are all well connected to London and the rest of the country by train and bus services, as is Manningtree, close to Cattawade, on the Stour and Orwell Walk. For information on train times call National Rail Enquiries on 0871 200 4950 or look on the internet – www.nationalrail. co.uk. For coach and rail transport to Suffolk from London and elsewhere, contact National Express

Lowestoft, at the northern end of the Suffolk Coast Path, is Britain's most easterly town (SCP, Stage 1)

Felixstowe. Of the 12 stations between Lowestoft and Ipswich, and the five between Ipswich and Felixstowe, only Ipswich and Lowestoft are staffed, but tickets may be bought on board the train. There is adequate car parking at all the stations.

Small towns such as Southwold and Aldeburgh on the Suffolk Coast Path have reasonable bus connections to the walks' start and end points, but smaller places such as Dunwich, Chillesford, Snape and Chelmondiston have only infrequent bus services, and timetables need to be studied carefully in order to make the most of connections at the beginning and end of each stage.

Express (www.national express. com; 08717 818178) or visit their website. The East Suffolk Railway Line (www.eastsuffolkline.com) has regular rail services between Lowestoft and Ipswich that stop at stations fairly close to the coast, such as Saxmundham, Darsham and Woodbridge, and there is also a useful branch line between Ipswich and

Some local bus services, including the Suffolk Links Wilford (Demand Responsive Transport Service) between Woodbridge and the coast, need to be booked in advance the day before. A very useful facility for planning purposes is Traveline East Anglia (www.travelineeastanglia.org. uk; 0871 200 2233), which has links to timetables and route maps on its website.

By car, the Suffolk coast is easily reached from the rest of the country by taking the A12 between Ipswich and Lowestoft and turning off for the coast at the appropriate point. There are generally adequate car-parking facilities along the Suffolk coast, although the town car parks at Southwold and Aldeburgh can sometimes be full in high season.

FERRIES

Several stages of the walks involve the use of ferries – timetables should be checked beforehand, as the ferries are seasonal and do not run year-round.

On the Suffolk Coast Path the extension to the alternative Orford Loop (see Stage 6) makes use of the Butley rowing-boat ferry, which runs from Easter Sunday to the end of September. Stage 8 of the Suffolk Coast Path requires the use of the Deben ferry across the river from Bawdsey Quay to Felixstowe Ferry. It carries foot passengers and bicycles and usually operates daily between May and September from 10am to 6pm, and at weekends from Easter weekend to May and also in October from 10am to 5pm (£1.80 single and £2.50 return at the time of writing). At other times there may be a river taxi service (07709 411511).

The Landguard Fort to Harwich and Shotley Gate ferry service is used on the alternative shorter version (Stages 4 and 5 only) of the Stour and Orwell Walk. This runs 9.45am–5pm on weekdays, and 9.45am–5.35pm on weekends and school holidays, daily from 4 May to 26 September; it also runs at weekends from 10 April to 3 May and at Easter (www.harwichharbourferry.com; 07919 911440). It costs £5 for adults.

Southwold Pier, Britain's only 21st-century pier, was opened in 2001 (SCP, Stage 2)

WHEN TO GO

The busiest months on the Suffolk coast are July and August, especially during the English school holiday period. Services and amenities can become stretched at this time, especially in popular resorts such as Southwold and Aldeburgh. Overall, probably the most pleasant months to walk are May, June and September, although April and October both have their merits if the weather is good. Late spring is the best time to see wild flowers, and September is the ideal month for migrating birds, although late April and May are probably better for seeing (and hearing) migrant warblers including nightingales. Characteristic shingle flora such as sea pea and yellow-horned poppy are at their flowering peak in July and August.

For walkers hiking the entire length of the Suffolk Coast Path, the main seasonal limitation is the need to use the ferry service between Bawdsey and Felixstowe (Stage 8). This operates only at Easter weekend, and then between May and October. At other times of the year it is necessary to make a very long detour around the River Deben estuary. Similarly, anyone wishing to make use of the Butley ferry on the Orford Loop alternative (Stage 6 of the Suffolk Coast Path) must undertake this section between Easter and the end of September, when the ferry is running.

None of the routes in this book is so long that it makes the limited daylight hours of winter an issue. Walking coastal Suffolk in winter has, in fact, its own, perhaps rather bleak, charm. The Stour and Orwell Walk especially is rewarding during the winter months, as both estuaries are home to large numbers of wildfowl and waders at this time of year.

WHAT TO TAKE

Suffolk coastal weather is generally mild, with little snow in winter and a cooling breeze in summer. As with any route, walkers should check weather forecasts before setting out to determine whether wet-weather clothing is required for that day. Substantial boots and appropriate clothing should be worn, and a small, comfortable daypack containing additional clothing, waterproofs, map, food, drink and a camera should be carried.

In summer, insect repellent is a good idea as midges may be a nuisance along some stretches of coastline; mosquitoes can also be a minor problem in some areas of woodland. On brighter days sun cream may be necessary, as walkers are often unaware of getting burned because of the cooling effect of a sea breeze. A sun hat is also advisable.

FOOD AND ACCOMMODATION

Food is often available at pubs and cafés close to the start and end points of many walk stages, although, as there are one or two exceptions to

Fishing boats and bathers on the beach at Dunwich (SCP, Stage 4)

the rule, it is always a good idea to carry a supply of food and drink and 'emergency rations' in case of delay or exceptional circumstances. Places where refreshments are available are listed in the box at the start of each walk stage.

For those wishing to walk these routes in their entirety, stopping overnight along the way, there is plenty of accommodation available at the larger towns such as Lowestoft, Ipswich, Woodbridge and Felixstowe, as well as a good number of hotels and B&Bs at resorts including Southwold, Walberswick and Aldeburgh, although these tend to be in great demand in high summer and it is wise to book well ahead. The smaller villages, where some stages start or finish, tend to have far

less choice on offer – suggestions are given in the box at the start of each stage. Most of the tourist information centres listed in Appendix B can help find accommodation and assist with booking, as well as provide timetables of local transport.

WAYMARKS AND ACCESS

All the routes are generally well signed and clearly waymarked. The Suffolk Coast Path is marked with a yellow arrow on a blue disc. The alternative route in Stages 6–7, the Orford Loop, is signed 'Suffolk Coast Path: Orford Loop', and the Butley ferry variation of the Loop is signed 'Suffolk Coast Path: Orford Loop via Ferry'. The Stour and Orwell Walk is waymarked with a yellow arrow on a grey disc and the legend 'Stour and Orwell Walk'. The Sandlings Walk is marked with a rectangular plaque that has an arrow and a stylised nightjar symbol. Some older signposts have the same nightjar symbol etched into the wood. The text indicates where the way is unclear or signs may be hard to spot.

SAFETY

There are only a couple of serious dangers that walkers need to be aware of. Being cut off by the sea at high tide is a potential hazard along a few stretches of the coastal route, and it is essential that tide tables are checked carefully beforehand if the intention is to take the beach-walking option. These can be found online at www. tidetimes.org.uk or obtained from local tourist information centres.

Another potential danger is that of walking along narrow country roads where there is no pavement. The routes described in this book avoid that situation wherever possible, and in some cases fairly considerable detours are followed as a result of this. Nevertheless, there are some stages that involve a degree of road walking, and the wearing of bright outer layers in order to be seen in poor light is advisable.

MAPS

Three Ordnance Survey Landranger maps (1:50,000 scale) and four Ordnance Survey Explorer (1:25,000 scale) cover the routes.

OS Landranger
- 134 Norwich & The Broads
- 156 Saxmundham, Aldeburgh & Southwold
- 169 Ipswich & The Naze

OS Explorer
- OL40 The Broads
- 231 Southwold & Bungay
- 212 Woodbridge & Saxmundham
- 197 Ipswich, Felixstowe & Harwich

USING THIS GUIDE

The three long-distance walks in this guide have been broken down into manageable stages chosen for their convenient length (5–12 miles/8–19km) and, where possible, the availability of transport and facilities at, or close to, the beginning and end of each stage. These are merely guidelines, however; the suggested stages may be added together – or further divided – according to personal requirements. Suggestions have been made in the text where two stages may be combined in a single day for more energetic walkers.

At the start of each stage is a box summarising information about the route. Grid references have been given to accurately locate the start and end point of each stage – read the 'eastings' (the numbers horizontally across the map) first, followed by the 'northings' (the numbers listed vertically).

The timings given in the box are based on the speed of a walker of average fitness. The weather is unlikely to have much impact on the time taken to walk these routes, although a strong wind will no doubt slow things down slightly.

Tidal considerations are also mentioned in the box where appropriate. There are one or two sections along the Suffolk Coast Path where a high tide may prevent further advance and hold walkers up for a short period of perhaps ½hr to 1hr. Alternative inland routes are offered that can be used when it is high tide at the coast.

Each stage has an accompanying Ordnance Survey map extract that should be adequate to provide an overview of the route, but is not intended as a substitute for the relevant OS map itself, which walkers should also take with them. The routes described here are all covered by the OS 1:50,000 Landranger series, although – should more detail and route information be required – the OS 1:25,000 Explorer equivalent can be utilised instead; the relevant maps are listed in the box at the start of each walk stage.

In the description of each stage of the route, key features that appear on the OS map are shown in **bold** type to help with navigation.

The Meare and the House in the Clouds in Thorpeness (SCP, Stage 5)

THE SUFFOLK COAST PATH
Lowestoft to Felixstowe (55–60 miles/89–97km)

The Suffolk Coast Path follows the shingle beach near Bawdsey (SCP, Stage 8)

STAGE 1
Lowestoft to Covehithe

Start	Lowestoft, East Point Pavilion (TM 547 925)
Finish	Covehithe, St Andrew's Church (TM 523 818)
Distance	9 miles (14.5km) by inland route; 7 miles (11km) by beach route
Time	3–4hrs by inland route; 2½–3hrs by beach route
Maps	OS Landranger 134, 156; OS Explorer OL40, 231
Accommodation	Lowestoft (hotels, B&Bs); Kessingland (B&Bs)
Refreshments	Lowestoft (pubs, cafés); Kessingland (pub); Wrentham (pub)
Public transport	Lowestoft has a frequent train service to Norwich and Ipswich, both of which have good connections to London. Anglia Bus X2 service connects Lowestoft with Beccles and Norwich, while Anglia Bus 601 and 99 services link the town with Southwold, passing through Wrentham, the closest available transport to the finish point at Covehithe.
Note	Tide tables should be consulted before setting out (www.tidetimes.org.uk or TIC Lowestoft). For walkers following the beach route the most critical point is at Pakefield, where a high tide might reach right up to the cliffs and impede further progress. There is an escape route here onto private land at a holiday park.

This first stage of the Suffolk Coast Path might be considered the least engaging part of the entire route, although it is not without its points of interest. It soon leaves the bucket-and-spade trappings of Lowestoft and Kessingland behind, with the prospect of the more charming coastal towns of Southwold and Aldeburgh lying ahead.

There is a choice of beach or inland route, and this will be largely determined by the tide – at low or mid-tide it is preferable to stick to the beach between Lowestoft and Kessingland, while at high tide it is advisable to use the inland route that follows a busy main road for part of the way. Energetic walkers might wish to combine this walk with Stage 2 in order to complete the stretch between Lowestoft and Southwold in a single day.

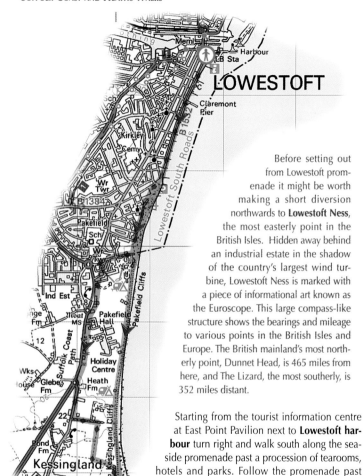

Before setting out from Lowestoft promenade it might be worth making a short diversion northwards to **Lowestoft Ness**, the most easterly point in the British Isles. Hidden away behind an industrial estate in the shadow of the country's largest wind turbine, Lowestoft Ness is marked with a piece of informational art known as the Euroscope. This large compass-like structure shows the bearings and mileage to various points in the British Isles and Europe. The British mainland's most northerly point, Dunnet Head, is 465 miles from here, and The Lizard, the most southerly, is 352 miles distant.

Starting from the tourist information centre at East Point Pavilion next to **Lowestoft harbour** turn right and walk south along the seaside promenade past a procession of tearooms, hotels and parks. Follow the promenade past **Claremont Pier**, where there is a clean, award-winning sandy beach and a concrete beachside walkway lined by a continuous terrace of brick beach huts. Continue along the promenade to the Centre for Environment, Fisheries and Aquaculture Science (CEFAS) office block, where there are steps down to the beach.

map continues
on page 36

Lowestoft Ness, Britain's most easterly point

Head along the path next to the fence, then walk across a grassy area towards a car park and around a corner to reach All Saints' and St Margaret's Church with its square tower, thatched roof and sundial above the porch. This is the parish church of **Pakefield**, effectively a southern suburb of Lowestoft. At the corner of the graveyard, by the track, find a Suffolk Coast Path waymark sign.

At low or mid-tide from here you can walk south from here along the beach either to Covehithe, as described in this stage, or as far as Southwold at the end of Stage 2. However, at high tide it will be necessary to follow the route that leads away from the sea. This is described below.

Following the inland route, go past the Oddfellows public house and a line of benches facing out to sea. There are boats beached on the shingle here and views back to Lowestoft harbour and the huge wind turbine beyond at Lowestoft Ness. Walk past a field that has a collection of beach huts and along a tarmac path with holiday chalets on the right. At the junction with the neighbouring holiday village, where there is a footpath sign pointing along Pakefield Cliffs and a Suffolk Coast Path sign pointing inland, take the latter, heading up a lane past Cliftonville residential cul-de-sac. Go straight on at the junction along Arbour Lane, and continue past the holiday park and a McDonalds to reach a roundabout.

The next section of a mile or so (1.6km) is not particularly pleasant walking, following a section of the busy A12. Go left along London Road towards the next roundabout and, just before reaching this, bear left along Catherine Terrace and Barnard Terrace, where a sign on a telegraph pole reassures that

you are still on the Suffolk Coast Path. Cross the rounda-bout, past an 'Ipswich A12' sign and the entrance driveway to **Pakefield Hall**. At the next roundabout, bear left along the **B1437** towards Kessingland.

Passing woods on the left and a row of terraces on the right, soon come to a road on the left with a caravan park sign. Turn left along this road and, near the reception centre, bear right then shortly right again along a path (no sign) between a field and a wooded area. Turning a corner, the tall square tower of Kessingland's St Edmund's Church comes into view. The path continues between open fields parallel to the beach. Go past a footbridge over a ditch to the right and continue to the end of the field, at which point turn left following the Suffolk Coast Path sign. At the end of the path, where there is a house on the left, take the rough track to the right, which just after a footpath leading to the beach turns into a tarmac road with bungalows. Continue parallel to the beach, passing an information board on Kessingland parish, and then turn left along a narrow footpath next to a hedge and down steps to the beach where you turn right.

> **Kessingland**, once the summer residence of the novelist H Rider Haggard, consisted of two separate communi-ties – Kessingland Beach and Kessingland Street – until the 1960s. The village is now a popular holiday centre with several holiday parks and an Africa-themed wild-life park, Africa Alive!

The beach at Kessingland is a wide, windy expanse, where in high summer a number of specialist plant spe-cies such as sea kale, sea pea, sea holly and yellow-horned poppy are to be found growing among the shingle. ▶ Walk along the shingle for a little less than 1½ miles (2.4km), past a holiday village at Kessingland's southern edge, until reaching a fenced-off pumping sta-tion outfall at Benacre Ness. Between the outfall and the large brick pumping building pass through a gate that leads into Benacre National Nature Reserve, managed by English Nature.

Parts of the beach are barred to dogs between 1 May and 30 September, so dog walkers should use the promenade as an alternative.

St Andrew's Church, Covehithe, a 17th-century church within a much larger, older church

Walk along the dunes with The Denes (a shallow flooded gravel pit) on your right, then immediately turn right along a track inland past **Beach Farm** and through a gate with another Benacre National Nature Reserve board. The track leads inland through large arable fields. Pass another track to the left that reads 'Permit holders only' and continue to a bend of a minor road, with Benacre church straight ahead. Turn left and follow the road, keeping left at the entrance to **Hall Farm**. After about 1 mile (1.6km) from the Hall Farm entrance, at a T-junction by a plantation, follow the track left (or turn right for Wrentham village, where there is a fairly frequent bus service to both Lowestoft and Southwold).

Continue along the track past mixed woodland on the right. Turn left at a junction with a minor road and follow this until it merges with another, with Church Farm and the partially ruined St Andrew's Church straight ahead. This is the hamlet of **Covehithe**, a once much larger settlement that has been dramatically reduced by erosion. To see evidence of this, continue along the road that passes the church and soon come to sudden halt where the road falls away to what is now the beach.

Walkers who have followed the beach route turn inland here for Covehithe. Even for those continuing all the way to Southwold along the beach, a short diversion from Covehithe Cliffs to the ruins of St Andrew's Church is worthwhile. Should the tide be close to shore at this point, it is also possible to use this as an escape route and then follow the inland route on to Southwold.

Almost all of the settlement of **Covehithe** has now vanished beneath the waves, a casualty of coastal erosion. A small, prosperous town in medieval times, Covehithe today is just a tiny hamlet. The once great church of St Andrew's was partly dismantled by villagers in the late 17th century when permission was given to remove the roof and build a smaller, more easily maintained place of worship within the original walls against the west tower. The tiny new church that dates from 1672 is thatched and houses the original medieval font. The tower of the older church still stands as a beacon to ships at sea, but, given the severe erosion that persists along this coast, it is unlikely that it will still be standing by the mid-21st century.

STAGE 2
Covehithe to Southwold

Start	Covehithe, St Andrew's Church (TM 523 818)
Finish	Southwold promenade (TM 511 763)
Distance	7 miles (11km) by inland route; 4 miles (6.5km) by coast route
Time	2½–3hrs by inland route; 1½–2hrs by coast route
Maps	OS Landranger 156; OS Explorer 231
Accommodation	Southwold (hotels, B&Bs)
Refreshments	Southwold (pubs, cafés); Wrentham (pub, minimarket)

Public transport	Anglia Bus 601 and 99 services run between Lowestoft and Southwold, passing through Wrentham, the closest available transport to the starting point at Covehithe. Southwold also has bus services to Great Yarmouth, Halesworth and Norwich, which in turn have regular direct train services to London.
Note	It is possible that storms might breach Benacre Broad or Covehithe Broad at some point in the future, which would make progress along the beach difficult or impossible. If in doubt, contact the Suffolk Coast and Heaths AONB at 01394 384948.

As with the previous stage, there are two alternatives depending on the state of the tide – a beach walk or an inland route. With a low or mid-tide, the beach route is probably preferable. It is usually possible to walk along the beach all the way to Southwold, although if the tide is threatening south of Covehithe Cliffs follow the inland route from Covehithe.

The inland route is described below, and has undergone considerable revision from the former route shown on earlier OS maps. The old route passed south of Easton Wood and used a short stretch along the B1127 north of Southwold. This new inland route is longer and detours inland some way, but is altogether safer and preferable.

At **Covehithe** church, walk back to where the two roads converge and there is a road sign pointing to Southwold and Wrentham as well as a waymark. Follow the left fork, ignoring the footpath to the left that is marked 'Suffolk Coast Path' on older editions of the OS map. Continue on to Crossways Cottages and cross Green Lane heading straight on. This continues across fields to reach the **B1127** opposite Hitcham's Lane. Turn left along the road and follow the wide roadside verge for a short distance to **South Cove**, where a track leads off to the right.

Follow this past farm buildings to **Frostenden Corner**, then turn left past cottages to soon reach another minor road, where you turn right alongside woodland. Continue

due south along a track at the corner where the road turns right towards **Vale Farm**. Ignoring a track that curves away to the left, carry straight on until meeting a minor road, Wash Lane, and turn left to head south along it. Take the next track to the left, Smear Lane, and follow this for a few minutes before turning sharp right along a track that heads south past **Reydon Grove Farm**. This soon reaches a narrow road, where you turn left and continue past **The Elms Farm** and a junction to the right before reaching the junction at **Reydon Smear** by a house. This is Smear Corner, where the original inland route of the Suffolk Coast Path is rejoined.

Reaching a road junction with a speed limit sign, head straight across into **Reydon** along Covert Road. Just before arriving at the next junction there is a group of interesting almshouse cottages on the right.

Just after the wheat harvest, near Covehithe, in high summer

The **Reydon almshouses** bear the date 1908 and the inscription 'The Rest for the Aged' and have some attractive architectural features including crow-step

gables. It is recorded that English composer Ralph
Vaughan Williams, an active member of the Folk
Song Society, cycled over to the Reydon almshouses

The splendid almshouses at Reydon were built in 1908

in October 1910 to collect two songs from Charles Newby, one of the almshouse's first residents, who had formerly been a publican and coal merchant in the town.

Turn left at the next junction then immediately take a waymarked footpath to the right. This shady path soon emerges into an area of grazing that has views of Southwold. Go over a stile towards the beach ahead, along a path squeezed between two hedgerows, to reach the car park. Go past the boating lake on the right and the pier on the left to follow the promenade into the town centre.

Southwold, with its old-fashioned genteel atmosphere, is considered by many to be one of the most charming coastal towns in all England. It received a town charter from Henry VII in 1489 but virtually all of the town's original buildings were destroyed in a fire in 1659 and a consequence of this was to leave open areas known as 'greens' as firebreaks in the subsequent rebuild.

Today, Southwold's most notable sights are its pier, dating from 1900 but fully restored and reopened in 2001, a white lighthouse dating from 1887 that stands in the centre of the town, the Adnams Sole Bay Brewery and the imposing 15th-century St Edmunds Church with its exquisite roof that holds numerous wooden angel figures. The colourful beach huts that line the promenade are another of the town's most iconic sights – these come at a hefty asking price, as does any real estate in this, one of the most expensive of Suffolk towns.

STAGE 3
Southwold to Dunwich

Start	Southwold promenade (TM 511 763)
Finish	Dunwich, Ship Inn (TM 478 706)
Distance	6½ miles (10.5km)
Time	2½–3hrs
Maps	OS Landranger 156; OS Explorer 231
Accommodation	Southwold (hotels, B&Bs); Walberswick (B&Bs, holiday lets)
Refreshments	Pubs and cafés in Southwold, Walberswick and Dunwich
Public transport	Southwold has bus services to Great Yarmouth, Lowestoft, Halesworth and Norwich, the latter of which has regular connections to London. Dunwich has very limited public transport – two buses a day Monday to Saturday (Nightingales of Beccles 196 service), one mid-morning and one early afternoon, to Leiston; and one early afternoon to Saxmundham, which has a station on the East Suffolk Railway Line. Leiston and Saxmundham are both connected to Ipswich by bus, with onward rail and coach connections to London.
Note	If the footpaths between Walberswick and Dunwich are closed (for conservation work, etc), follow the signs for the Sandlings Walk (ie follow Sandlings Walk Stage 7, below, in reverse). A rowing-boat ferry (seasonal) links Southwold and Walberswick and saves a couple of miles.

This walk has plenty of variety – the genteel seaside delights of Southwold, with its pier, lighthouse, promenade and splendid pubs; the more workaday charms of the Blyth estuary, with its fishing huts and boat piers; Walberswick, a long-gentrified fishing village; and Dunwich, once a large, important port, but now almost completely lost to the North Sea. Marshes, shingle beaches and forest along the way make for a pleasing mix of landscapes in between the village attractions.

Although it may usually be possible to walk all of the way along the beach between Walberswick and Dunwich, it is not to be recommended – it is very hard going walking on shingle all the way, and there is the possibility that the shingle bank may be breached by the sea in the future.

Begin at **Southwold** promenade in front of the lighthouse. Just beneath the promenade lies one of Southwold's most iconic sights, its brightly painted beach huts, which are highly prized and change hands for considerable sums of money. The sloping bank above them is covered in cel-ery-like, lime-green alexanders in spring. The road curves round into the centre, but go straight along the path past

Southwold is well known for its beach, lighthouse and iconic beach huts

45

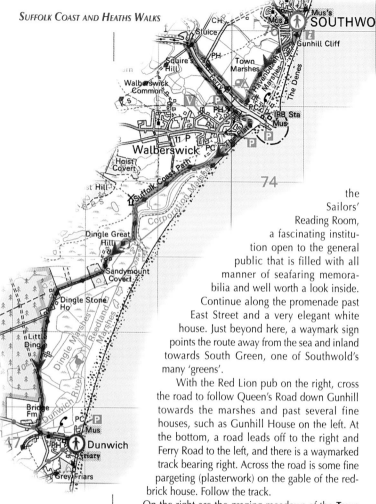

the
Sailors'
Reading Room,
a fascinating institu-
tion open to the general
public that is filled with all
manner of seafaring memora-
bilia and well worth a look inside.
Continue along the promenade past
East Street and a very elegant white
house. Just beyond here, a waymark sign
points the route away from the sea and inland
towards South Green, one of Southwold's
many 'greens'.

With the Red Lion pub on the right, cross
the road to follow Queen's Road down Gunhill
towards the marshes and past several fine
houses, such as Gunhill House on the left. At
the bottom, a road leads off to the right and
Ferry Road to the left, and there is a waymarked
track bearing right. Across the road is some fine
pargeting (plasterwork) on the gable of the red-
brick house. Follow the track.

On the right are the grazing meadows of the **Town
Marshes** and soon, on the left, is a grassy area with three
benches facing out over the meadows and a nightjar
sculpture that indicates that this stretch also coincides
with the final section of the Sandlings Walk. Follow the
track, with a raised bank on the left. Before long, there

are glimpses of the black-painted fishing huts of the River Blyth estuary ahead, and the houses of Walberswick beyond. After passing another bench, the path goes through a short stretch flanked by trees before emerging at the raised bank above the road that leads northwest along the Blyth estuary. A hut offering boat trips is on the left, and a little further up is the rowing-boat ferry that links Southwold and Walberswick and saves a couple of miles for those in a hurry. ▸

The coastal path continues northwest along the right bank of the estuary. It is a picturesque, ramshackle area with lots of boat-centred activity, landings and miscellaneous nautical fixtures and fittings. There are several huts selling excellent fresh fish along here, as well as a sit-down fish and chip shop, a tearoom and, just before the Bailey bridge, the **Harbour Inn pub**.

Cross the Bailey bridge to the other side of the River Blyth. Waymark signs indicate that this point is at the confluence of two routes: the Suffolk Coast Path and the Sandlings Walk (its final stretch before leading into

The Walberswick ferry runs daily between 10am and 5pm, Easter holidays and June to September, and weekends only in May and October. It cost just 80p (bicycles 80p, dogs free) at the time of writing.

Fishing huts along the Blythburgh estuary in Southwold

A derelict windmill in Walberswick marshes

Southwold). Follow the path next to the estuary southeast towards Walberswick. This side of the river is much quieter, with none of the industry found on the Southwold bank.

Walberswick was an important trading port between the 13th and early 20th centuries, at first a rival to, and then taking over from, Dunwich, when that port was lost due to silting at the end of the 13th century. Around the close of the 19th century the village was chosen as an artistic base by the English Impressionists led by

Philip Wilson Steer, and the Scottish architect Charles Rennie Mackintosh also came here to live and paint watercolours in 1914. The artistic tradition lives on, with a number of luminaries of British cultural life owning holiday homes in and around the village.

The path leads to some black wooden fishing huts and a large car parking area. Turn right here across **The Flats** and follow the sign over a footbridge across a creek that is sometimes busy with children and parents heading towards some dunes. Go along a path beside a fence towards more beach huts. There's a gap in the dunes towards the beach, but carry on over a bridge towards another car park and turn right towards a camping area. Follow the path behind the dunes until a finger-post points inland past a couple of pools and to a footbridge, where there is a sign leading through bird-filled reedbeds next to a dyke. All manner of bird sightings are possible along here – you may catch a glimpse of bearded tits and sedge and reed warblers in the reeds, and even be lucky enough to see a marsh harrier overhead.

Eventually the path reaches a red-brick uncapped windmill, after which it leads to the left. A little further on another finger post points to the right around **Dingle Great Hill**, a name that, with the best will in the world, seems something of an exaggeration. At a large area of woodland, a grassy path with plenty of wild flowers and butterflies leads alongside it on the left-hand side. Where the path splits, take the left turn towards Dingle Great Hill Farm. A gate leads straight ahead along a wide track through the dense woodland of **Sandymount Covert**, which is composed almost entirely of sycamore with some oaks. As the path emerges through the other side there are good views to the right over the marshes towards Walberswick.

The track, lined by gnarled old hawthorns, continues towards Dunwich Forest and soon, looking to the left, Dunwich becomes visible for the first time. The track follows the eastern edge of **Dunwich Forest** past Little Dingle Cottages and Sole Bay Lodge. Continue over a cattle grid and, eventually, after passing some farm buildings with a 'Residents only' and bridleway sign and a large barn conversion, turn left towards Dunwich's St James's Church on the main road. Follow the road past the church and museum to reach the **Ship Inn** and, just beyond, a car park behind the beach that has a café with outdoor tables that is locally famous for its fish and chips.

Dunwich, now little more than a small Suffolk village, was once a much larger and far more important place. As the largest port in East Anglia by the mid-13th century, it once boasted at least five churches, two hospitals, two monasteries and a guildhall, in addition to several shipyards. Earlier, in the Saxon period, Dunwich (originally 'Donmoc') had been the centre of the East Anglian bishopric before this moved to North Elmham in Norfolk in 870.

Storms in the 13th and 14th centuries swept away many village houses, and ongoing coastal erosion further reduced the village over the following 200–300 years. The few ruins that stand today – the remains of the Franciscan priory and the leper hospital of St James – once stood a mile inland. All Saints' Church, the last of Dunwich's ancient churches, was finally lost to the sea in the early 20th century, and its remains now lie underwater just offshore. Local legend tells of church bells being heard out to sea on stormy nights, although this has never been substantiated. St James's, the only church now standing in the village, is relatively new, having been built in 1832.

For those wanting to know more about Dunwich's fascinating history, there is an excellent local museum on St James Street, near the Ship Inn, that is open between April and September.

STAGE 4
Dunwich to Thorpeness

Start	Dunwich, Ship Inn (TM 478 706)
Finish	Thorpeness, The Meare car park (TM 472 595)
Distance	8 miles (13km)
Time	3–3½hrs
Maps	OS Landranger 156 Saxmundham, Aldeburgh & Southwold 1:50,000; OS Explorer 231 Southwold & Bungay 1:25,000 and OS Explorer 212 Woodbridge & Saxmundham 1:25,000
Accommodation	Thorpeness (hotel, holiday lets)
Refreshments	Dunwich (pub, café); Thorpeness (pub, cafés); Dunwich Heath NT visitor centre (café)
Public transport	Dunwich has limited public transport (see Stage 3). Thorpeness has four buses a day (Nightingales of Beccles 521 service) to and from Halesworth via Darsham and Saxmundham, and these places all have rail stations on the East Suffolk Line. Thorpeness also has morning buses to Ipswich on schooldays, and links to Rendlesham and Wickham Market (with connections to Ipswich) using the Coastal Accessible Transport Service (www.cats-paws. co.uk) that must be booked the day before (01728 830516). Aldeburgh, just south of Thorpeness, has regular bus services to Woodbridge and Ipswich.
Note	There is a point just before Thorpeness that is impassable at high tide, but there is an alternative inland route that leads to Thorpeness.

This stage entails a pleasant mix of inland and coastal walking, with large stretches of heath, woodland and shingle beach. It also passes two of this coastline's most notable features – the flagship RSPB reserve at Minsmere and, virtually next door, the nuclear power station of Sizewell B. Indeed, it is the iconic giant golf ball of the power station that dominates the horizon for much of this walk.

Beginning at the Ship Inn in **Dunwich**, walk towards the sea and go around the corner to take the Westleton road to the right. Almost immediately a Suffolk Coast Path sign appears to the left that points along a permissive path through a spinney and behind houses close to the cliff edge. A little further on, a gate to the right leads through a field to the ruins of the **Greyfriars Friary**, a worthwhile short diversion. Continue south along the path, with the sea on your left, past remnants of old crumbling wall. The path soon curves around to the right alongside an ancient wall beside a field with a good view of the friary ruins. A gap in the wall leads through woodland, a fragmented part of Grey Friars Wood. Follow the waymarked path along a track past a fancy wrought-iron gate with friar figures. Pass several attractive cottages to reach another waymark indicating that the route goes straight on.

The ruins of 13th-century Greyfriars Friary are all that remain of the medieval town of Dunwich

The track soon merges with a road, which is followed until it reaches another private road to the left that has a footpath sign. Go along here, passing a few houses, and then go through a gate to follow a broad track through woodland, the larger portion of Grey Friars Wood. Cross

the track to the house and head straight on, with coniferous woodland on the right and deciduous trees on the left. Arrive soon at a minor road, the Minsmere Road, that leads to the bird reserve and Dunwich Heath.

map continues
on page 55

> **Dunwich Heath** is a large area of typical Suffolk coastal heath owned by the National Trust. This specialised habitat of gorse, heather and light sandy soil is home to bird species including Dartford warblers, nightjars and woodlarks, as well as adders and even the elusive but rare antlion.

Cross the road carefully to continue along a bridleway passing a sign reading 'National Trust Mount Pleasant Farm'. Go straight ahead along a track with hazel and hawthorn hedgerow on both sides until reaching a crossroads, where a waymark sign points left. Take this and follow the path south across Dunwich Heath. Continue through a vast area of heather and gorse that is alive with butterflies in summer to soon catch a first glimpse of the white golf ball of Sizewell B floating eerily on the horizon like a giant mushroom.

A little further on the single row of white terraced houses that make up the National Trust-owned coastguard cottages is visible. As the route climbs up slightly towards the coastguard cottages, the sea comes into sight once more. The path eventually emerges at a picnic area. Turn left at the barn study centre then right at the road to

Heather in bloom on the National Trust-owned Dunwich Heath

the car park that stands next to a **National Trust visitors' centre**. There is also a tea room and gift shop here, as well as toilet facilities.

Walk down the path from the car park towards the marshes of Minsmere RSPB bird reserve below. Follow the bank with the marshes on the right. After about ½ mile (800m) there is a path that leads right into the bird reserve. Continue on past an array of concrete sea defences that date from World War II to pass another entrance into the reserve at East Hide. The sandy path continues south past more concrete blocks and another covered walkway into the reserve, and to a small pond to the right behind barbed wire. Another footpath leads inland from a well-constructed red-brick sluice – **Minsmere Sluice** – and from here you can easily make out a ruin that is marked on the OS map as 'Chapel'. Carry straight on towards Sizewell. The path widens here and continues alongside marshes to the right.

The **Minsmere RSPB reserve** was established in 1947 when the Royal Society for the Protection of Birds leased 1500 acres of land from local landlords, the Ogilvie family. This land was purchased in 1977, and further purchases have been made in recent years to increase the size of the reserve to almost 10km².

Minsmere reserve is a mixture of several different habitats – reedbeds, open water, heath, grazing, scrub, woodland, dune and shingle – and such a wide diversity encourages a large variety of birds to breed on the reserve, with over 100 resident species and a further 240 migratory visitors recorded at the site. Avocets, the bird of the RSPB emblem, breed here in large numbers, and an estimated 30 per cent of the UK breeding population of bittern are also resident. Over 1000 moth and butterfly species have also been recorded at Minsmere, and a moth (Minsmere common underwing) previously unrecorded in Britain was discovered here in 2004.

Looking back there are fine views of the coastguard cottages and the ruined chapel, while ahead the Sizewell 'golf ball' looms increasingly large ahead. Keep a look out for marsh harriers over the reedbeds, a relatively common sight during the breeding season here. A line of concrete blocks and a track inland mark the position of the Sandlings Walk path, which follows the same route as the Suffolk Coast Path for a short distance in front of the power station. Close to Sizewell B, information boards tell of black redstarts and kittiwakes breeding at the power station – both

birds are well adapted to urban environments and, in this case, attracted by the building's convenient ledges and vast expanse of concrete. The dry sandy area just before reaching the power station has a good range of specialist plants such as harebells, vetches, lady's bedstraw and centaury. Close to the station it is possible to hear the thrum of the turbines within, a slightly eerie sound.

> **Sizewell B nuclear power station** is the second of two nuclear power stations to be built close to the Suffolk coastal village of Sizewell. Sizewell A, which opened in 1967 and was decommissioned in 2006, has two Magnox reactors, while Sizewell B, which came on stream in 1995 and is instantly recognisable because of its giant white 'golf ball', has a pressurised water reactor. A third power station at the site, Sizewell C, is currently being planned.

At the car park near the southern end of the power station it is possible to make out Thorpeness in the distance. Power station or not, the beach here is quite popular with local bathers and dog walkers, and some people keep boats here too. Next to the car park is a conveniently placed café that is open almost every day of the year.

Where the road to the car park bends around to the right, continue along the track past wood-boarded cottages and fishing huts and a caravan and camping park. The path continues beside a concrete wall and beneath an arch that forms part of the boundary of the once grand **Sizewell Hall** to the right that has 'Private property' signs. A path leads back down to the beach, but the Suffolk Coast Path continues along the concrete wall. Soon you will reach more steps that lead down to the beach.

It should be noted that dogs are banned on Thorpeness beach between May and September, so if you are walking with a dog at this time of year you should follow this brief diversion.

A path leading inland here provides an **alternative inland route** to Thorpeness should high tide be approaching (there is a point about 1 mile (1.6km) further on, just before Thorpeness, that is impassable at high tide). ◄ For this alternative route, turn left at the T-junction, then left again after about ½ mile (800m) to head south alongside a conifer plantation. This leads into Thorpeness, just north of the church.

Otherwise, the coast path continues, tightly squeezed between hedgerows in places, before dropping down just above the beach shingle. The shingle here has a huge amount of sea kale in addition to yellow-horned sea poppy. Be aware that at high tide this last stretch into **Thorpeness** may be impassable for a short period (see suggested detour above), but generally it is possible to continue and, if desired, turn right into the village to walk round the church and follow the road to The Meare car park.

STAGE 5
Thorpeness to Snape Maltings

Start	Thorpeness, The Meare car park (TM 472 595)
Finish	Snape Maltings (TM 392 574)
Distance	6½ miles (10.5km)
Time	2½–3hrs
Maps	OS Landranger 156; OS Explorer 212
Accommodation	Thorpeness (hotel); Aldeburgh (hotels, B&Bs); Snape (pub)
Refreshments	Pubs, cafés and restaurants at Thorpeness, Aldeburgh and Snape Maltings
Public transport	Thorpeness has buses to and from Halesworth and limited connections elsewhere (see Stage 4). Snape Maltings has buses to and from Woodbridge. Aldeburgh, close to Thorpeness, has regular bus service to Woodbridge and Ipswich.

This stage of the Suffolk Coast Path involves an enjoyable deviation away from the coast, a necessary detour given the presence of the wide estuary of the River Alde. Leaving Thorpeness, the route skirts the upmarket resort of Aldeburgh before heading west through woodland and heath to reach Snape

Maltings, a few miles south of the small market town of Saxmundham. Much of the route follows what is known as the Sailors' Path between Aldeburgh and Snape Warren.

Thorpeness was once simply a tiny fishing hamlet, but in 1910 the wealthy Scottish barrister Glencairn Stuart Ogilvie, who had bought up the entire area between Sizewell, Aldeburgh, Leiston and Aldringham, started to develop the village as a private holiday resort. Many holiday homes were built in mock Jacobean and Tudor styles, along with a country club, golf course, almshouses and an artificial boating lake (The Meare). The village's most notable building, the oddly elevated House in the Clouds, came about when it was decided that the village water tower would be an eyesore and so was clad with wood to disguise it as a dwelling.

The creation of The Meare was inspired by a regular visitor to the holiday village, JM Barrie, and some of its locations and landing stages take their names from *Peter Pan*, Barrie's most famous work. The Meare serves as the location for the Thorpeness Regatta in August, about the same time as the Aldeburgh Carnival held just down the road.

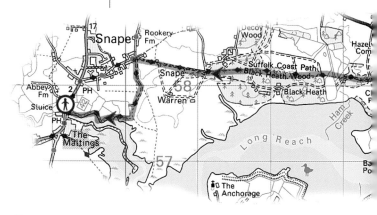

Boating on The Meare, the man-made lake at Thorpeness

From the car park by **The Meare** follow the signs that point back towards the beach. Go south along the way-marked footpath past a line of mock Tudor holiday homes until reaching **Haven House**, where the path goes through a grassy area between the beach and the road. After about ½ mile (800m) the path crosses the road next to an isolated house, then follows a track alongside North Warren RSPB reserve, where there are clear views of the windmill and the House in the Clouds at Thorpeness and of Sizewell B beyond. Anyone walking here in late April or May might also be lucky enough to hear nightingales singing in the hedgerows. Marsh harriers can also be seen displaying here in spring. Cross a path near a large belt of trees on the left and continue along a track past several houses until reaching a road, the busy B1122.

Aldeburgh, now a fashionable and rather upmarket resort, was once an important fishing and boatbuilding centre at the mouth of the River Alde. Like many places along this stretch of coastline, the town has for many years suffered from serious erosion. Much of the old town has been lost over the centuries – the ancient timber-framed Moot Hall that houses the town museum and stands by the shore was once located in the town centre. Despite its rather posh atmosphere and connections with the world-famous Aldeburgh Festival, the town is also famous for its fish and chips, with one of the family-run shops in the town being considered among the best in the country. Freshly caught fish can be bought at very reasonable prices from the fishermen's huts on the shingle beach.

Carefully cross the B1122, and the path continues through part of Aldeburgh golf course, where signs warn that walkers should exercise caution crossing the fairway. Follow the path through a rough mown area to cross the course, while being vigilant for flying golf balls. A gate leads onto a quiet residential road opposite the **Red House**, where Benjamin Britten and Peter Pears resided in the town from 1957 until their deaths. Turn right along Golf Lane, and continue with the links on your right and the outskirts of Aldeburgh on your left.

The English composer **Benjamin Britten**, although originally from Lowestoft further north, spent many years as a resident of Aldeburgh, setting up the still-thriving Aldeburgh Festival in 1948. His opera *Peter Grimes*, which used a libretto adapted from the work of local poet George Crabbe, concerned itself with the tragic life of a fictitious Aldeburgh fisherman. Britten died at home in Aldeburgh in 1976 and is buried in the church-yard of the town's St Peter & St Paul's Church alongside his life partner, the tenor Peter Pears.

Reaching the **A1094**, turn right. There is a footpath at first and then, after the Aldeburgh Golf Club clubhouse, a grass verge for most of the way, but be careful as traffic is fast here. After about ¾ mile (1.2km) turn off to a parking area at Hazelwood Marshes that lies just off the road to the left. From here as far as Snape, the Suffolk Coast Path follows the same route as The Sailors' Path, a popular local route.

The **Sailors' Path** between Aldeburgh and Snape is approximately 5 miles (8km) long. The path has three sculptural installations by Jonathan Keep, who draws his inspiration from the archaeology of the area, and the changing landscapes and lives of its inhabitants from Neolithic times. These were installed in 2008 and have been left *in situ* to deteriorate naturally. At a number of listening posts along the course of the route it is possible to hear local oral history recordings of life around the Alde estuary.

A boardwalk through Hazelwood Common on the Sailors' Path

Follow the track from the car park past a couple of cottages and then take the track off to the right that leads across marshes and past another house. From here, the track climbs slightly to give a good view of the estuary to the left. Continuing, meet a track to the right that leads to a house; ignore this and carry on left along a broad track following the waymark sign. The track drops down to the left to a house with a nature reserve sign, but continue straight on to go through a kissing gate to a wooded area. Go through this to continue past a derelict house in the wood and through a gate. **Hazelwood Common** lies to the right, as the path leads along a boardwalk through a marshy area and then across a meadow that usually has cows grazing.

After a further length of boardwalk and another bridge the route enters **Black Heath Wood** along a track that at first follows the edge of mature woodland of Scots pines, oaks, birches and other species. This eventually goes into the wood itself and leads past a terracotta sculpture erected in 2008 as part of a local arts project. On reaching a metal gate, go past some asparagus fields to the rights and birch woodland to the left to arrive at **Snape Warren**. The path soon brings you to a road corner on the edge of **Snape** village where there is a car park, a restricted byway heading right and a footpath heading left towards Snape village that is waymarked as the Sandlings Walk.

The Suffolk Coast Path leads due south from here towards Snape Warren Nature Reserve. Eventually, as the view of the reedbeds and estuary open up, the path veers right along the estuary towards the arts venue of Snape Maltings. The path meanders along a raised path towards the impressive complex of Snape Maltings ahead. On either side of the path are large expanses of reed that resonate with birdsong in spring and early summer. Looking east, it is possible to make out Iken church (marked on OS maps as 'The Anchorage') on the other side of the water. Reaching Snape Maltings, cross the bridge on the main road to turn left into the complex.

Snape Maltings, just south of the village of Snape, is a complex of converted 19th-century buildings originally used for the malting of barley for use in beer making. The Maltings closed in 1960, but has since been restored and converted into art galleries, craft shops and, most notably, a state-of-the-art concert hall that is the centrepiece of the annual Aldeburgh Music Festival initiated by Aldeburgh resident Benjamin Britten. In recent years, music studios and rehearsal rooms have been created from formerly redundant buildings, along with residential apartments around a communal garden. There is also an RSPB visitor centre, a weekly farmers' market and an annual food festival staged here.

Bird-rich reedbeds along the Alde estuary on the approach to Snape Maltings

STAGE 6
Snape Maltings to Chillesford

Start	Snape Maltings (TM 392 574)
Finish	Chillesford, junction at Hartford's Place (TM 387 522)
Distance	4½ miles (7.5km); via Orford Loop (to Chillesford or Butley ferry) 13½ miles (22km)
Time	2–2½hrs; via Orford Loop (to Chillesford or Butley ferry) 5–6hrs
Maps	OS Landranger 156 (Orford Loop also requires OS Landranger 169); OS Explorer 212
Accommodation	Snape (pub); Orford (hotels, B&Bs)
Refreshments	Snape (pub); Snape Maltings (pub, cafés, restaurants); Chillesford (pub)
Public transport	Snape and Chillesford both have buses services to and from Woodbridge, which has bus and rail connections to Ipswich and London.

It is mostly woodland and estuary that characterises this enjoyable stage of the Suffolk Coast Path, with the added bonus of a visit at the start to Snape Maltings with its various shops, cafés and concert hall. There is a slight chance that the boardwalk southeast of Snape Maltings may be flooded for short periods when there is a very high tide, which means you will have to wait a little while before setting off.

There is a choice of routes on this stage of the walk. About 1½ miles (2.4km) from Snape Maltings an alternative route, known as the Orford Loop, offers an extension to the Suffolk Coast Path. The Orford Loop heads eastwards then follows the River Alde south to Orford before rejoining the main route at Chillesford (at the end of Stage 6). An alternative version of the Loop continues on from Orford to use the seasonal ferry at Butley and rejoin the main route at the ferry landing stage near Burrow Hill (on Stage 7). Walkers on either route may want to stay overnight at Orford, where accommodation is available.

From the back of the car park at **Snape Maltings** a sign labelled 'Snape Explorer' leads to the continuation of the Suffolk Coast Path – alternatively, reach this same point directly from the road by taking a path that skirts The Maltings on its south side. The path soon joins a boardwalk (occasionally flooded – see above). Where the boardwalk ends there is a large plantation on the left, and the way follows a gravel path for a while before reaching a longer section of boardwalk with reedbeds on either side. Iken's St Botolph's Church soon comes into view – a fine diversion for those with plenty of time.

St Botolph's Church at Iken, marked on OS maps as The Anchorage, stands at a point where there was once an island and is very probably built on the site of St Botolph's seventh-century abbey. A large stone cross, discovered in the wall of the church tower, is of Saxon origin and carved with the heads of dogs and wolves, symbols associated with St Botolph, an English abbot who died in 680 and is a patron saint of travelling and farming. The cross is probably ninth century, and may have been erected to commemorate the destruction of the original monastery by Viking raiders.

On reaching **Ikencliff** picnic site go straight across the car park and carry on along the public footpath close to a hedgerow, eventually passing a cottage the right. The path soon comes to an open area with excellent views of the estuary. Continue walking more or less alongside the estuary, passing moored boats, holiday apartments and sea lavender growing in the mudflats, to get a fine view of Iken's St Botolph's

Church ahead. Soon you reach signs pointing the way for the Orford Loop, but unless you wish to take this alternative longer route (see below) ignore these and instead take the steps that lead south away from the water.

ALTERNATIVE ROUTE – THE ORFORD LOOP

This offers an extension of the Suffolk Coast Path that takes in more of the River Alde and the pretty village of Orford. A variation continues on from Orford and uses the seasonal ferry at Butley to rejoin the main Suffolk Coast Path at the Butley ferry landing stage, near Burrow Hill (Stage 7). The route is not marked on OS maps, but is clearly waymarked on the ground.

To Chillesford

Instead of heading south just before **Iken Hall** (TM 403 561) carry on east in front of the hall to join a road. Turn left, then at the junction turn right (left is to Iken church). Follow this southeast next to Iken Marshes, and past two more road junctions and **Hill Farm** before turning right just before High Street and **Stanny House Farm**. After about ½ mile (800m) take the second road left past a plantation and **Cowton House** to reach a raised riverwall. This continues northeast for a while before turning sharply south at a promontory and following the **River Alde** south for 5–6 miles (8–9.5km) to arrive at Orford Quay.

From Orford Quay, walk into **Orford** village and then fork left at the northern edge of the village to follow a track that leads northwest past Sudbourne Hall to **Chillesford**, where the Orford Loop rejoins the main route at the end of Stage 6 (and start of Stage 7), close to the **Froize Inn** pub and restaurant.

Detour via the Butley ferry

If the Butley rowing-boat ferry is operational (Easter Sunday to the end of September), then instead of going into Orford it is possible to continue south along the river from **Orford Quay**, cutting the corner at **Chantry Point** and heading inland about ½ mile (800m) on from Chantry Point across **Gedgrave Marshes**. Turn left at the road to go past **Gedgrave Hall** before turning right along a farm track after a plantation. This leads to the bank of the **Butley River**. Turn left and walk along the river to reach **Butley ferry** after about 10mins. Once across, the main Suffolk Coast Path can be rejoined at Burrow Hill and followed south to eventually reach **Shingle Street** (see map, Stage 7). Shingle Street is still a long way, though – walkers who decide to make use of the Butley ferry route might be better off using Orford village as a starting point.

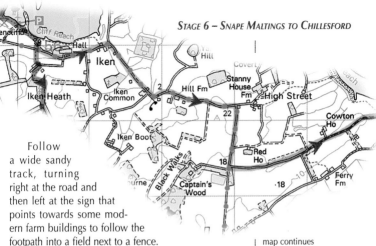

Follow a wide sandy track, turning right at the road and then left at the sign that points towards some modern farm buildings to follow the footpath into a field next to a fence. The path swings left in front of a large modern barn, then turns right to lead along a track next to a field towards a stand of conifers. Continue due south, with the wood to the right and fields to the left, to reach a gap between the two wooded areas, then continue in the same direction alongside another belt of trees, with the trees on

map continues
on pages 68–69

A field of sunflowers, close to the village of Chillesford

the left and a large arable field on the right. At the edge of the tree belt turn right along the waymarked path that has fields on the left and a belt of trees on the right.

Leaving the edge of the plantation continue straight on, dropping slightly to reach a road. Cross this to enter Tunstall Forest, where you immediately meet a track along which you turn right. Very soon after this (look out for a waymark that may be covered in bracken) another track leads left – follow this, heading south through Tunstall Forest away from the road. Reaching a wider woodland ride continue straight on, and a little later, as the main track swings around to the right, take the path to the left through a younger plan-tation area before

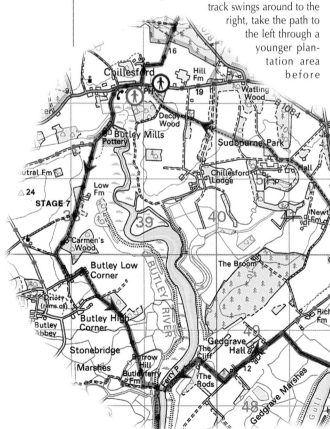

it widens out in an area of mature Scots Pines. Keep heading south, crossing another couple of tracks to reach the **B1078**, a fairly busy road that passes through the forest, which you should be able to hear before seeing it.

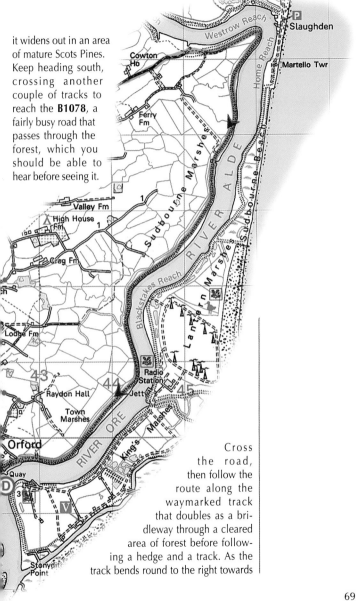

Cross the road, then follow the route along the waymarked track that doubles as a bridleway through a cleared area of forest before following a hedge and a track. As the track bends round to the right towards a farm, take the track to the left towards the houses of Chillesford village, which is by now visible. Go past a pair of thatched cottages that have a date of 1851 on them. At the junction turn left and head south towards the main road that has the highly regarded **Froize Inn** pub and restaurant close to the junction. Turn right to walk into Chillesford village.

Chillesford has a number of buildings, including the church tower, built from locally made red crag bricks. A 20m (60ft) skeleton of a whale was once found in the old village brickyard. Presumably, the animal swam up the Butley River before expiring. There was also once a famous polo ground here, but this was ploughed up in the 1950s following the death of the owner, who was trampled during a game.

STAGE 7

Chillesford to Shingle Street

Start	Chillesford, junction at Hartford's Place (TM 387 522)
Finish	Shingle Street, car park (TM 370 431)
Distance	8 miles (13km)
Time	3–4hrs
Maps	OS Landranger 156, 169; OS Explorer 212, 197
Accommodation	Shingle Street (self-catering only); Butley Priory (guest house)
Refreshments	Chillesford (pub-restaurant); Hollesley (pub)
Public transport	Chillesford has a bus service to and from Woodbridge, which in turn has bus and rail connections to Ipswich and London. Shingle Street has a bus link to Woodbridge using the Coastal Accessible Transport Service (www.cats-paws.co.uk) that must be booked the day before (see Stage 4).
Note	There is nowhere for refreshment along this route other than at Chillesford, at the beginning, and Hollesley, a couple of miles inland from Shingle Street, at the end.

The charm of this stage of the Suffolk Coast Path is its isolation – in fine weather it can be sublime. Walking this route involves long, lonely stretches beside water, first alongside the Butley River and then beside the River Ore as it merges into the North Sea. Marshes feature prominently, too, as does the mysterious sand spit of Orford Ness, visible across the water. The route finally ends at Shingle Street, little more than a row of houses that face out to sea.

Starting at the junction at Hartford's Place in **Chillesford**, by the post box and bus shelter, follow the Suffolk Coast Path south along the lane opposite. After walking for about 5mins pass a mill on the right that has been converted into holiday apartments, then continue past more houses and **Butley Mill** studios on the left, and a partly hidden mill pond to the right. As the road forks take the waymarked farm track to the left. This soon opens up to give broad, expansive views across arable fields and Rendlesham Forest to the west. Pass a group of farm buildings and a pine plantation and continue straight, ignoring another track that joins from the right. Passing **Carmen's Wood** and an isolated house notice Butley church to the west above some trees.

Continue past a belt of trees to reach a crossroads, then turn left past cottages and bungalows to reach **Butley Low Corner**, where the road turns at a right angle to head south. At the next junction, keep left to follow the track alongside the right-hand side of a wood. Continue past a small break in the trees and a track to the left to pass a second piece of woodland, then go along the farm track through fields that may have cattle towards a low hill. Continue through a gate and over a stile to climb up **Burrow Hill,** from where there is a good view of the Butley River, the River Ore estuary and the North Sea beyond. Looking back there is a pleasing vista of Rendlesham Forest and the farmland that you have just traversed. Go over another waymarked stile and diagonally down the hill through a gap in the hedge to reach a farm track. Here turn left to reach a gateway that leads up the bank to the landing stage for Butley ferry. ▶

See map on pages 68 and 73

The Orford Loop continuation route (see Stage 6) rejoins the main Suffolk Coast Path route here.

A signpost with Suffolk Coast Path waymarks, near Butley ferry

The **Butley ferry** between the Capel and Gedgrave banks of the Butley River, which claims to be the smallest licensed ferry in Europe, is a rowing-boat ferry operated by local volunteers. It runs between Easter and the end of September (11am–4pm) on weekends and bank holidays. The ferry costs £1.50 per person, £1 for children and £1.50 for bicycles (at the time of writing) and can take up to six passengers at a time; it may be pre-booked by phoning 07913 672499.

Go south along the bank with the **Butley River** on your left. Continue over a sluice and past a roofless brick structure at Boynton Dock to head southeast towards the confluence of the Butley and Ore rivers. By now it should be possible to make out the pylons and 'pagodas' on Orford Ness to the northeast. The path soon veers due south opposite **Dove Point**, the southernmost extremity of Havergate Island, an RSPB reserve. Passing another old concrete defensive structure, the path swings around to the southwest to follow the narrow channel of the **River Ore**, with the southern tip of Orford Ness opposite.

Orford Ness is a designated National Nature Reserve of considerable ecological importance, as it is the largest vegetated shingle spit in Europe. Now owned by the National Trust, which runs a regular ferry service across to it from Orford Quay, it was formerly a top-secret military site used in both world wars and in the subsequent Cold War period. The Atomic Weapons Research Establishment used the site for testing detonators, and the distinctive 'pagoda' buildings used for this purpose can still be seen. The numerous masts at the northern end of the spit are used for broadcasting the BBC World Service.

The path continues along the raised bank next to the River Ore, past grazing marshland and occasional defensive structures, until it passes a sign announcing 'Hollesley Marshes Nature Reserve' to the right. The path continues to follow the bank, apart from one short section that deviates briefly inland, and eventually the open sea and a row of white cottages at Shingle Street come into view

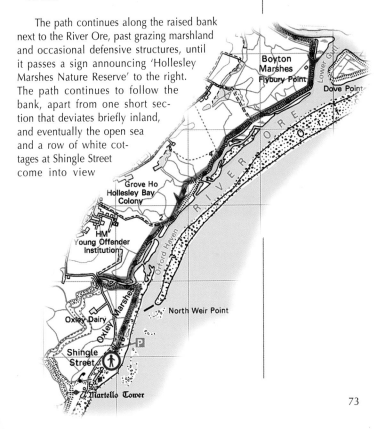

The raised bank along the River Ore looking north

Hollesley, with its pub, minimarket, HM Young Offender Institution and occasional buses to Woodbridge, lies a couple of miles inland from Shingle Street along the road by the bridge.

ahead. On meeting the curve of the tributary at **Orford Haven**, the path leads sharply around to the right away from the sea, where there is another sign for Hollesley Marshes Nature Reserve.

Follow the river as far as the bridge. There is an option here to take the shorter, more direct route along the road into Shingle Street or, alternatively, follow the road south briefly before heading towards the sea again on the path on the southern bank of the tributary. This soon turns sharp right to lead along the edge of Oxley Marshes into **Shingle Street**, a hamlet that these days boasts just a car park, a telephone box and a fine shingle beach rich with sea kale, yellow-horned poppy and other maritime salt-tolerant plants. ◄

Shingle Street was once a fishing hamlet that also served as a coastguard station and home to River Ore river pilots. There used to be a pub here, the Lifeboat Inn, but this was destroyed in World War II, when it was used to test a newly developed bomb from Porton Down. There were also lurid reports of a failed German invasion here after the inhabitants were evacuated in 1940. These subsequently proved to be false, but were probably encouraged at the time for purposes of propaganda. It is possible that, if sea defences are not strengthened, the hamlet could disappear into the sea within the next 20 years.

STAGE 8
Shingle Street to Landguard Fort, Felixstowe

Start	Shingle Street, car park (TM 370 431)
Finish	Landguard Fort, Felixstowe (TM 283 320)
Distance	10½ miles (17km)
Time	4–5hrs (excluding ferry crossing waiting time)
Maps	OS Landranger 169; OS Explorer 197
Accommodation	Felixstowe (hotels, B&Bs)
Refreshments	Felixstowe (pubs, cafés); Felixstowe Ferry (pub, cafés); Landguard Fort (snack van)
Public transport	Shingle Street has a bus link to Woodbridge using the Coastal Accessible Transport Service (www.cats-paws.co.uk) that must be booked the day before (see Stage 4). Felixstowe has regular bus and rail connections to Ipswich. Landguard Fort has an hourly bus service to Felixstowe and Ipswich. The river ferry between Bawdsey Quay and Felixstowe Ferry operates at weekends Easter and October, and daily from May until the end of September.
Note	The alternative inland route avoids a tough 2-mile (3.2km) stretch on a shingle beach. There is one point on the coastal route, close to Bawdsey Quay, which may be impassable for a short time at high tide.

The most important thing to note when planning this stage is that it involves catching a ferry between Bawdsey Quay and Felixstowe Ferry, which operates only at weekends at Easter and in October, and daily from May to September. At other times of year it will be necessary to detour around the Deben estuary – a major inconvenience, especially on the Bawdsey side, where public transport is at a premium. A better option during the no-ferry season might be to make a long day of it by combining Stage 7 with the first part of Stage 8 as far as Bawdsey, and from there backtracking to Hollesley (near Shingle Street), where there is public transport.

From **Shingle Street** car park walk south in front of the row of cottages before turning inland at the end of them just in front of the Martello tower. Follow the bridleway behind the bungalow along a narrow track fenced on both sides, then take the track to the right that leads diagonally across a meadow to reach a raised bank. Turn left, and then left again when it reaches another raised bank that has a drainage channel on its right-hand side. Follow the path in a southerly direction towards more Martello towers in the distance.

Martello towers were constructed during the early 19th century at a time when Britain was concerned about a possible invasion by Napoleon. Stretching around the southeast coast from Seaford in Sussex to Aldeburgh in Suffolk, the towers made up a chain of just over 100 defensive fortifications designed to protect the English coastline. Others were built in Ireland, the Channel Islands, Scotland and elsewhere in British territories. These two-storey garrisons, up to 12m high with thick, cannon-resistant walls and a platform for artillery, never saw active service against Napoleon, although some were put to use as anti-aircraft units during World War II, and others were used by HM Coastguard against smugglers. 47 have survived – some are preserved as historic monuments, while others have been converted to private residences or are derelict.

Continue south along the path past two Martello towers and a number of ponds on the left. Eventually reach the beach car park at **Bawdsey**, where there is a series of four large rectangular ponds next to a road that are usually filled with wildfowl, as well as a concrete World War II gun emplacement just before another Martello tower. Head inland along East Lane, past **East Lane Farm** on the left, then reach a junction with a school. Turn left at the junction, pass the school and then go left at the road. Walk south along the road past **High House**, a three-storey Georgian farmhouse, and **Bawdsey Hall**, with a high Leylandii hedge until reaching a finger post pointing left along a track towards the sea. For the coastal route, take this path across fields and descend down some steps to the shingle

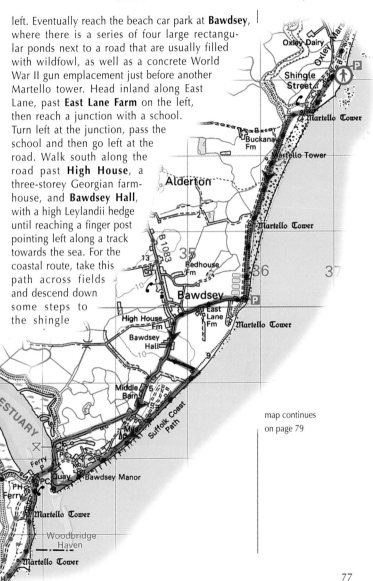

map continues
on page 79

A Martello tower – one of the most northerly in the country – south of Shingle Street

you do not want to walk along shingle for a tough 2 mile stretch (3.2km), then continue instead along the road to rejoin the main route at Bawdsey Quay – take care of motor traffic and be aware that visibility is not good along this road in poor light.)

The Suffolk Coast Path continues south along the shingle beach all the way to Bawdsey Quay. This is quite tough going, but enjoyable and rewarding because of its quiet isolation – you may be close to Felixstowe at this point, but you would hardly know it, apart from the occasional sight of container ships out to sea. Walking south, pass through a minimalist seascape of sea, sky and shingle, with lines of blackened and eroded groynes jutting out to sea and sandy cliffs that have sand martin nest holes in places. The beach here is rapidly eroding, and there is one point close to Bawdsey Quay where the tamarisk bushes come right down to the beach, and it may be impassable for a short period of time at high tide.

At a point where there are steps down to the beach – and probably a couple of boats – there is a waymark sign attached to one of the wooden groyne posts. A further sign points the path away from the groynes to pass close to the base of the cliff where there are 'private' signs for the Bawdsey estate. Continue above the beach along a raised shingle path past foundations and defensive walls to the right.

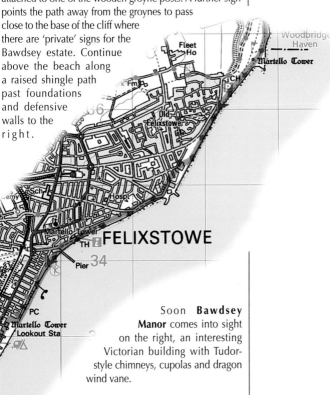

Soon **Bawdsey Manor** comes into sight on the right, an interesting Victorian building with Tudor-style chimneys, cupolas and dragon wind vane.

Bawdsey Manor, close to the mouth of the River Deben and built between 1886 and 1895 as a residence for Sir William Cuthbert Quilterbut, was purchased and used

79

The visitor centre at Bawdsey Quay operates May to September, as does the café. The ferry service across the River Deben runs during these months, and also at weekends at Easter and in October.

as an RAF radar research station during World War II. The house remained under RAF ownership as a training school until purchase by the Toettcher family in 1994. Bawdsey Manor is now used for wedding receptions and various residential courses. The former transmitter block serves as a museum, with limited opening hours.

Continue close to the fence, which swings round to the right to offer some good views of the manor. As the mouth of the River Deben comes into view, Bawdsey Quay and Felixstowe Ferry, across the water, both suddenly reveal themselves. ◄

The Bawdsey ferry operates from Easter until October, taking passengers and bicycles across the River Deben to Felixstowe Ferry. In the early 20th century a steam-drawn chain ferry operated here, but this was replaced by a launch between 1931 and the start of World War II, when the ferry closed to the public. A daily service, contracted by RAF Bawdsey, operated from the end of

Houses at Bawdsey Ferry look across the River Deben to Felixstowe

World War II until 1974, since when the service has operated in the summer months only.

From **Felixstowe Ferry**, where there is a café, pub and a couple of huts selling fresh fish, head briefly along the road before climbing concrete steps to the left just before a bus stop. Follow the waymarked path south along the seawall towards a Martello tower ahead, passing in front of a rather elegant row of terraced houses before going past the tower. Looking back from here, there is an excellent view of Bawdsey Manor across the mouth of the Deben. Continue past a line of beach huts until a second Martello tower comes into view. ▸ Carry on along the seawall, passing signs asserting that the southern end of the golf course is private property. Continue underneath long lines of beach huts until reaching a point where a procession of groynes runs out to sea and the coast bends around to the right at Cobbold's Point.

If, for any reason, this path is closed, there is an alternative path that goes through the golf course to reach this tower, although the seawall route is preferable.

After passing a red and yellow lifeguard's hut, the coast road runs almost up to the seawall. Pass another line of beach huts, and at the beginning of the last block of these, close to the point where the coast bends round to the right, take the steps up to the right that lead up through beach huts to a public toilet block and Golf Road. Turn left past some mock Tudor houses, and then left at the next junction. With North Cliff Court on the left and a very tall ornate brick wall on the right, the sea soon comes into view again as the road drops down to rejoin the seawall promenade, from where there is an impressive view of the cranes of The Port of Felixstowe far ahead.

Continue walking the promenade alongside Undercliff Road East past the Fludyer Arms and nursing home to go past more beach huts. After a toilet block, reach the beginning of a line of stone groynes on the beach; here, on the hill above, look out for a very grand building that was once Felixstowe's Bartlet Hospital, a convalescent home built on the site of a former Martello tower. After passing more beach huts, a pleasant park and the Spa Pavilion theatre, the pier becomes visible ahead

It should be noted that dogs are not allowed on the stretch of beach south of here between May and September.

and, beyond that, the cranes of the port. ◀ Just before the **pier**, with the Felixstowe Leisure Centre next door, is a tourist information centre on the right. The cranes of Felixstowe docks loom ever larger to the south – a fascinating sight.

> **Felixstowe**, sitting at the end of a peninsula between the Deben, Stour and Orwell rivers, is both a seaside resort and a port, the largest container port in the United Kingdom. In the past the town has hosted dignitaries such as Kaiser Wilhelm II and TE Lawrence ('of Arabia'), and Wallis, Duchess of Windsor (Mrs Simpson) spent time here while awaiting the abdication of Edward VIII, her future husband.

The next stretch along the promenade is dominated by customary holiday resort trappings – amusement arcades, ice cream kiosks, fish and chip shops and cafés. On the road on the right pass an unusual, brightly painted art deco building with four towers that now operates as an amusement centre. Just beyond this to the

Felixstowe Ferry at the mouth of the River Deben

right is Beach Station Road, which follows the route of the Stour and Orwell Walk. Continue south past a car park and more beach huts towards another Martello tower. Continue along the promenade past the Martello tower, now a **coastguard lookout station**, and turn right across a parking area to a row of terraced houses and turn left.

Follow the road south past a caravan park until reaching the car park at Landguard Common. Take the track across the common, which runs parallel to the road hugging the perimeter fence of the container park, until it reaches the road leading to the Landguard Nature Reserve car park that curves around **Landguard Fort**.

Landguard Fort, at the mouth of the River Orwell, came into being in 1543 under Henry VIII, when two short-lived blockhouses were constructed at the present site. A new fort was built in 1628, and repaired and fortified in 1666 under Charles II. This was attacked unsuccessfully by Dutch marines in the following year. A new brick fort was built in 1717, which was subsequently replaced by another pentagonal structure in 1744, the walls of which remain to this day. Further remodelling and additions took place in the late 19th century, and the fort served as barrack accommodation through the 20th century until 1956, when it was abandoned as no longer having any military function. English Heritage took over the fort in 1997 and opened it to the public after structural repair work. Although it is now officially in Suffolk, Landguard Fort was considered to be part of Essex during the 18th and 19th centuries.

Follow the road round to the right just above the fort and on to a small car park at the viewpoint. There is a conveniently placed caravan snack bar here, and the car park is often filled with sightseers. Superb views can be had from here across to Harwich in Essex and also to Shotley Gate. This marks the end of the Suffolk Coast Path and, for those keen to continue their tour of the Suffolk coast, the beginning of the Stour and Orwell Walk.

THE STOUR AND ORWELL WALK

Felixstowe to Cattawade (42½ miles/68km)

A lonely boat in a creek on the Shotley Marshes (S&O, Stage 4)

STAGE 1

Landguard Fort, Felixstowe to Nacton

Start	Landguard Fort, Felixstowe (TM 283 320)
Finish	Nacton, St Martin's Church (TM 217 397)
Distance	10 miles (16km)
Time	4–4½hrs
Maps	OS Landranger 169; OS Explorer 197
Accommodation	Felixstowe (hotels, B&Bs)
Refreshments	Landguard Fort (snack van); Felixstowe (pubs, cafés); Levington (pub)
Public transport	Felixstowe has regular bus and rail connections to Ipswich. Landguard Fort has a bus service to Felixstowe and Ipswich. Nacton has an hourly bus service to Felixstowe and Ipswich.
Note	An alternative route (½ mile/800m) avoids the main railway crossing in Felixstowe.

The Stour and Orwell Walk begins where the Suffolk Coast Path ends – at Landguard Fort at the mouth of Harwich harbour, where both the Stour and Orwell rivers open out to the North Sea. This first section of the walk begins in a very industrial setting – first leading around the lengthy perimeter of the Port of Felixstowe container terminal, before passing through the far more peaceful terrain of the Trimley Marshes nature reserve and alongside the north bank of the River Orwell, before finally venturing inland to the village of Nacton, just southeast of Ipswich.

ALTERNATIVE ROUTE – BY FERRY TO SHOTLEY GATE

Rather than walking from Landguard Fort, the Stour and Orwell Walk can be made much shorter by making use of the seasonal passenger ferry between Landguard Fort and Shotley Gate via Harwich. Using this dramatic short-cut, only the second part of Stage 4 and Stage 5 are walked – a route that could even be covered in one long stage.

Starting at **Landguard Fort** car park, walk briefly along the road on the northern side of the fort before turning left to follow the footpath across Landguard Common that runs parallel to the perimeter fence of the container terminal. On reaching another car park, walk across it and follow the road north towards Felixstowe, past a caravan park and a row of terraced houses, before skirting to the right at the junction just before a Martello tower that now serves as a **coastguard lookout station**. Turn left at the seawall promenade past some beach huts. From here there are good views ahead to Felixstowe and Felixstowe Ferry beyond. Continue straight ahead until reaching a car park and large brick toilet block; cross the main road and head inland west along Beach Station Road.

The Port of Felixstowe is Britain's largest container port and the fourth largest in Europe, dealing with up to 20,000 containers per month. With easy access to the open sea and water as deep as 13m (43ft), tankers and container ships of up to 180m (590ft) are able to dock here. The docks first began to grow after World War II, when they were bought up for development by a Norfolk corn merchant.

Fishing at Landguard Fort, next to the cranes of The Port of Felixstowe

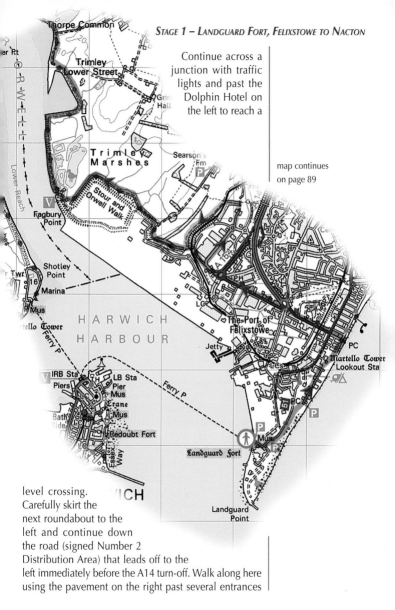

Continue across a junction with traffic lights and past the Dolphin Hotel on the left to reach a

map continues on page 89

level crossing. Carefully skirt the next roundabout to the left and continue down the road (signed Number 2 Distribution Area) that leads off to the left immediately before the A14 turn-off. Walk along here using the pavement on the right past several entrances to docks and container parks. (**Warning:** be very wary of lorry traffic along this section of the walk.) Pass a modern glass building on the right and, on reaching the next roundabout, follow it around to the left to walk along Fagbury Road. Once again, be wary of container port traffic, especially as there are usually few pedestrians around this part of town. Continue past yards filled with containers piled high and another busy entrance into the port. Reaching the **railway crossing**, go left through the gate to cross the line. (**Note:** freight trains to and from the port can cause long delays here – if you cannot cross because the gates are closed, you might want to consider the inland route diversion outlined below).

ALTERNATIVE ROUTE – AVOIDING THE MAIN RAIL CROSSING

Return briefly back along the road towards Felixstowe and turn left along Parker Avenue. Follow this for about ½ mile (800m), then cross a roundabout and continue along a minor road, turning left along a footpath just after a wooded area. This crosses the railway track, which is carefully traversed. Then follow a footpath and track south alongside the railway line to rejoin the Stour and Orwell Walk path just west of the railway gates.

The view here is one completely dominated by the relentless and noisy comings and goings of the container port – quite a sight to behold but not necessarily a place to linger.

Cross the railway line through the yard and go through the opposite gate. The path here that skirts a wooded area can be muddy after rain, but soon improves as it bends gently uphill to the right. Soon the path reaches a green area with a bench that marks the **viewpoint** at Fagbury Cliff. ◄ From here the path descends again through woodland to reach an open area of arable fields and hedgerows. The path soon swings right along a farm track at the edge of a field with a line of oaks on the right and woodland on the left. At the edge of the wood, a waymarked track to the left leads west towards Trimley Marshes nature reserve. Trimley railway station, a convenient hub for transport connections at the beginning or end of a walk, is 1½ miles (2.4km) northeast from here.

Follow the broad track west alongside wide open fields, and a ditch on the right and a fence and trees on the left. The path bends right and left, and while Felixstowe's container terminal may temporarily be out of sight it will probably still be audible, as will trains on the Ipswich to Felixstowe line that runs parallel to the north. After walking for 10mins or so a gate is reached with a sign announcing 'Trimley Marshes Nature Reserve'. Continue on along the main track around a sharp turn to the left past stands of willow as the huge cranes of the western limit of the container port come into view once more.

The Suffolk Wildlife Trust reserve at **Trimley Marshes** was created from arable land in 1990 as an attempt to mitigate the loss of mudflat habitat at Flagbury when The Port of Felixstowe was expanded. Traditional grazing is used to manage the wet meadows, and water levels are controlled by means of sluices, creating ideal conditions for wintering widgeon and Brent geese, and for breeding oystercatchers, redshank and avocets in summer.

On meeting a track that goes left to the container port and right towards the

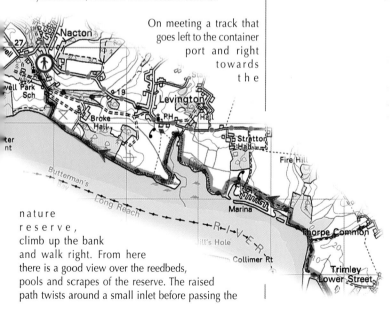

nature reserve, climb up the bank and walk right. From here there is a good view over the reedbeds, pools and scrapes of the reserve. The raised path twists around a small inlet before passing the reserve's **visitor centre** and a series of wooden bird hides ahead. There is a good open view from here across to the other bank of the River Orwell at Crane's Hill – a rare bit of elevation in this mostly horizontal landscape. The white masts of the marina at Levington can also now be seen straight ahead. After passing the northern limit of the nature reserve continue along the raised path past open pastures on the right until reaching a large wooden post painted black and white, where the raised bank swings sharply around to the right.

Although shown as a continuous line north on older OS maps, this next section involves a circle inland, as the bank has been purposefully breached here to create a large lagoon. Follow the path away from the river, which after 5mins or so curves north parallel to a line of electricity pylons. From here it is possible to see the extent of the breach of the original seawall path. Walk past a sandy island, probably full of waders, gulls and wildfowl, and a stand of dead trees, and on reaching a small wood follow the bridleway to continue straight on towards the marina ahead. The path passes through trees for a short while before following a hedge and fields, then climbs up slightly before dropping down through a copse. Ignoring the bridleway to the right that leads to Trimley St Martin, carry straight on past a sign for the Trimley Estate to reach a large **lake** on the right called Loompit Lake.

Levington's St Peter's Church, as seen from the Orwell shore

Follow the track alongside it, past the lake and a beach on the left to cross a concrete causeway. At low tide the difference in height between that of the river and that of the lake will be quite noticeable here. After turning a corner the path goes around the corner of the lake and then left through woodland. Continue behind the **marina** along the path that passes the dry dock and then climbs up through woods to pass a boat park on the right and fence on the left. Reaching a gate, cross the road just below a barrier to head into another boatyard. Take the signed footpath past buildings on the left to follow the line of trees, then cross another yard and more buildings to turn left along a line of trees behind the boatyard. The track bends right at the river's edge to meander alongside a marshy area to the right and saltmarshes purple with sea lavender (and full of waders in season) on the left. Looking inland, Levington's St Peter's Church with its brick tower can now clearly be seen atop a low hill.

In the early 19th century **Levington** village was a centre for digging coprolite – fossilised dung from prehistoric animals that has useful fertilising properties. The coprolite was dug by hand from just beneath the surface, washed and then processed locally for use in the fields. Although the industry has long since declined, a road in Ipswich still bears the name Coprolite Street. Levington Creek was once a working harbour, where coal was landed prior to World War I.

A couple more tracks join from the right and Levington Lagoon is passed before the path veers inland around the inlet of Levington Creek. At the head of the inlet, a road leads up the short distance to Levington village, which has an excellent pub and a decent bus service to Ipswich and Felixstowe. Otherwise, cross the sluice and continue along the west side of the inlet. Soon pass another footpath to the right that leads up to the church, continue south across another sluice to reach the mouth of the inlet, and turn right to walk past another footpath that leads inland.

Levington Lagoon, owned by the Suffolk Wildlife Trust, was created during the damaging east coast floods of 1953 when a breach was made in the sea wall. It is now one of the best places on the Orwell for bird watching, with estuarine specialities such as greenshank, spotted redshank, ruff and dunlin present on passage and during winter.

Follow the track west along and slightly above the estuary to enter the southern fringe of an attractive area of mature woodland with views of the water through tress below. The track drops gently out of the wood to cross an open clearing with several benches. In view behind are sheep pasture and parkland and the very grand Georgian building of **Broke Hall**. On reaching a wall and a track away from the water to the right, follow the track through a car park and alongside the boundary wall of **Orwell Park School** to reach a gate house and private drive. Continue left past the main entrance of the school – a grand Georgian building with its own observatory – to arrive at Nacton's St Martin's Church.

Silver evening light on the Orwell estuary at Levington Creek

The origins of the village of **Nacton** can be traced back to 1010, when Earl Ulfketel fought off invading Danes and the dead were buried in the tumuli at Seven Hills, just north of the village by the present-day A14. Two large estates dominate the village – Orwell Park, the seat of Admiral Vernon, famous for introducing the grog ration to the British Navy, and Broke Hall, established by Sir Richard Broke, the Lord Chief Baron of Henry VIII. The only pub in the village, the Anchor, was closed down during World War I by the owner of Orwell Park School.

STAGE 2
Nacton to Orwell Bridge, Ipswich

Start	Nacton, St Martin's Church (TM 217 397)
Finish	Orwell Bridge east bank (TM 178 403) or (via Ipswich Loop) west bank (TM 167 402)
Distance	4 miles (6.5km) to Orwell Bridge; Ipswich Loop an extra 5–6 miles (8–9.5km)
Time	1½–2hrs to Orwell Bridge; Ipswich Loop 2–2½hrs
Maps	OS Landranger 169; OS Explorer 197
Accommodation	Ipswich (hotels, guesthouses)
Refreshments	Ipswich (pubs, cafés, restaurants)
Public transport	Ipswich is well connected by bus and rail. Nacton has a bus service to Ipswich and Felixstowe.
Note	Crossing the Orwell Bridge on foot may not be to everyone's taste, and it is occasionally closed to pedestrians; in these circumstances, take the 'Ipswich Loop' through the town.

This stage offers two alternatives – the more direct route to the western bank of the River Orwell that makes use of the Orwell bridge (in Stage 3), and a route that follows the 'Ipswich Loop' and avoids the bridge. Although the

Ipswich Loop adds another 5–6 miles (8–9.5km) to the overall length of the Stour and Orwell Walk, it does allow for a visit to Suffolk's county town to see its sights and make use of its numerous facilities.

Starting at St Martin's Church in **Nacton**, walk north alongside a wall and past the impressive gates of Orwell Park Lodge to reach a T-Junction. Turn left, and soon after continue around a corner to the right past a private drive that leads off left. The next section is a fairly lengthy stretch along the old Ipswich to Felixstowe road, which is wide, straight and quite busy with traffic. There is no footbridge, but a grass verge and good visibility ahead make for safe, if not particularly enjoyable walking. Continue along the road past open fields to the left and a view down to a wooded valley to the right. Soon the busy A14 dual carriageway comes into view (and earshot) ahead.

On approaching the hectic road junction it is

best to transfer to the left hand side of the road to avoid traffic from the right around a blind corner. Take the footpath on the left next to the fence just before the first of the two roundabouts. Walk along this and then very carefully cross the approach road keeping to the combined footpath and cycle track. Walk under the **A14 flyover**, turn left then carefully cross the slip-road coming the other way and continue ahead. Almost immediately you arrive at a 'Welcome to Ipswich' sign.

> **Ipswich**, Suffolk's county town, has Anglo-Saxon origins, and the town centre is laid out in a typical Anglo-Saxon road pattern. Ipswich was once an important port and famous for its ship building, but its quays began to silt up in the 18th century. A deep-water channel was dredged in 1946 to enable it to continue as a port, although it is unable to cope with boats the size of those that berth in the Port of Felixstowe. One of the town's most iconic sights is the 18th-century Ancient House in the Buttermarket area of the town centre, which is one of the finest examples of pargeting (decorative plaster work) in the country.

Continue along the footpath for a short distance until reaching a road coming from the left that is signed 'Orwell Country Park'. Turn left and follow the route along here past an attractive half-timbered house and, a little later, a concrete pillbox. Keep to the road, which veers slightly left and right, until reaching a car park and private road ahead. Turn left to walk across the **bridge** over the A14. Once across, take the road to the right that runs at first parallel to the dual carriageway until reaching a sign for **Orwell Country Park**. Turn right to walk through a car park, and then turn left down a shady path next to an enormous oak tree, one of many over 400-year-old trees in this remnant of ancient woodland owned by Ipswich Borough Council. The path drops steeply through birches and pines until, just before a private property sign, another waymark points left through a green gate and along a path that crosses an open grassy area. Turn right at the next crossroads of paths to walk through more woodland and over concrete steps across a boggy area to soon reach the Orwell shore. Follow the path – heavily eroded in places – towards the looming Orwell Bridge passing meadows on the right.

> The **Orwell Bridge**, opened in 1982, towers nearly 40m (130ft) above the river of the same name. With a span of 1287m (over 4200ft), it is among the ten longest concrete structures in the world.

The Orwell Bridge close to Ipswich, over 1km long, is one of the ten longest concrete structures in the world

The path goes alongside a river beach at one point, and at high tide this might be impassable for a short period. Cross over some concreted outflow pipes and climb up and slightly away from the river towards the bridge. Just after passing underneath the bridge reach a waymark post that offers two options – 'The Stour and

Orwell Walk' directly across the bridge or the 'Ipswich Loop' that avoids it by making a detour through the town. Turn right to walk across the **Orwell Bridge**, or keep straight on to go into **Ipswich** through Orwell Park.

ALTERNATIVE ROUTE – THE IPSWICH LOOP

Ignore the sign pointing right towards the Orwell Bridge and continue in the same direction, climbing uphill to the right towards an open grassy area. Carry on through **Pipers Vale**, through trees to where another track joins from the left, and on through a gate. At the gate turn left past warehouses to reach the corner at the bottom of a cul-de-sac – Raeburn Road. Head along Raeburn Road, passing a school to reach a main road – Landseer Road – and then turn right to walk past All Hallows, a modern brick church, on the left. At the traffic lights turn left along Clapgate Lane. After passing Benacre Road on the right, and the block of flats at Reydon House on the left, turn left into Landseer Park.

Follow the path through the park that hugs the northern boundary and passes mostly through a belt of woodland. Passing close to the bottom of Dereham Avenue keep going, veering sharply to the right, then left, then right again on the path that keeps close to the park boundary and garden fences. Eventually arriving at Cliff Lane, go through the gate to the road, cross over and go left down the hill almost as far as the junction with Landseer Road. Just before the junction turn right through a gate into **Holywells Park** and follow the path, sometimes muddy following rain, north through woodland and alongside ponds and a stream. Carry on past a gate into an open area, and go through an area of mature trees and more ponds to reach a metalled path. Turn left and go through the gate to leave the park.

Turn left down Myrtle Road and then right at the roundabout at the bottom along Duke Street. Walk along Duke Street past industrial units and new development. Pass Coprolite Street on the left to arrive at traffic lights. Turn left to pass some half-timbered buildings on the left and modern buildings on the right. Recent development on the left, such as Neptune Square, gives access to a waterfront promenade and revamped dock frontage. Pass more jettied, timber-framed buildings to reach the Lord Nelson Inn and Fore Street on the right that leads into the pedestrian zone of the town centre. Keep left to follow Salthouse Street, which merges into Key Street and later College Street. Pass some interesting old wharf-side buildings and the Customs House. On the right is the Church of St Mary at the Quay and then

The Haven Marina at Ipswich

a heavily eroded gateway to an ancient college. Just before the roundabout, the Church of St Peter's by the Waterfront has an interesting wrought-iron gate in its entrance porch. Turn left just before the roundabout to cross the **River Orwell** along Bridge Street.

Almost immediately after crossing the bridge turn left down Dock Street, which continues to follow the river along Stoke Quay past converted maltings as far as the Steamboat pub, where it becomes New Cut West. On reaching Bath Street, turn right, and then left at the roundabout, and second left at the next one to follow the A137. This continues for some distance as Wherstead Road. Just before Bourne Bridge, continue straight over the roundabout and follow the footpath to the left that separates from the road before turning left again along the **B1456** in the direction of Orwell Bridge. Arriving at the **marina**, turn left to follow the riverwall route to pass underneath the bridge, from where you can rejoin the Stour and Orwell Walk from the west side of the bridge as described in Stage 3.

STAGE 3
Orwell Bridge, Ipswich to Pin Mill

Start	Orwell Bridge east bank, Ipswich (TM 178 403)
Finish	Pin Mill, near Chelmondiston (TM 206 380)
Distance	10 miles (16km)
Time	3½–4hrs
Maps	OS Landranger 169; OS Explorer 197
Accommodation	Ipswich (hotels, guesthouses); Chelmondiston (B&B)
Refreshments	Pubs at Pin Mill and Chelmondiston
Public transport	Ipswich is well connected by rail and bus with the rest of the country. Pin Mill is close to Chelmondiston, which has regular bus services to Ipswich and Shotley.

This stage of the route begins with a crossing of the Orwell Bridge. Once the bridge has been traversed, the route offers pleasingly varied walking, and it may come as a surprise to find such attractive, almost sleepy countryside so close to the hurly-burly of Ipswich. Pin Mill, with its excellent pub, is an ideal place to round off a walk. For those who have completed the Ipswich Loop outlined in Stage 2, the route begins at the second paragraph on the west side of the bridge.

Starting beneath the **Orwell Bridge**, facing north, take the waymarked path to the right that goes over a stile and leads underneath the bridge to its southern side, where steep steps lead from a gate up to the bridge walkway. Once on the bridge, it takes 15–20mins to traverse it. There are excellent views along the estuary to the left, although the constant thunder of traffic, much of it container lorries en route to Felixstowe port, will probably discourage much lingering on the bridge itself.

On the western side of the bridge, steps leads off to the left down the bank to a field, from where a footpath leads across it in a southeasterly direction parallel to the estuary. This crosses a minor road before continuing between fields in the same direction to reach another road

Freston Wood is filled with bluebells and wild garlic in spring

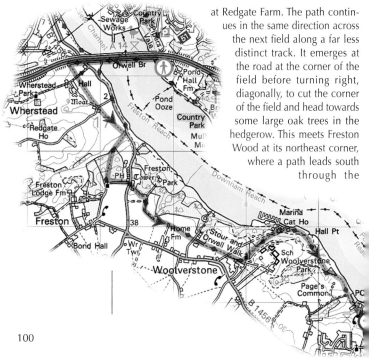

at Redgate Farm. The path continues in the same direction across the next field along a far less distinct track. It emerges at the road at the corner of the field before turning right, diagonally, to cut the corner of the field and head towards some large oak trees in the hedgerow. This meets Freston Wood at its northeast corner, where a path leads south through the wood towards the southwest corner of the wood close to Freston's church. The path through the wood is indistinct in places – taking the right-hand fork when other paths converge should ensure that you eventually emerge at the right point.

Freston Wood is an ancient wood with species that include hazel, oak, alder, ash and sweet chestnut, as well as many wild flowers, birds and butterflies. Its lower reaches are carpeted with wild garlic (ramsons) in spring, while a little higher up there is an impressive bluebell display in May.

Emerging from the wood, turn left along the road past the entrance to St Peter's Church, well worth a short diversion.

Freston's **St Peter's churchyard** holds an unusual wooden war memorial – a life-size representation of 'Peace' holding a laurel wreath that was originally sculpted from oak in 1921 and restored and rededicated on Armistice Day 2006. The church interior was

'Peace', a wooden war memorial in Freston St Peter's churchyard

ruined by the 19th century, but restored during the Anglican revival of the late Victorian period. Only the font remains from medieval times.

Walk a short distance along the road to the junction, passing some wonderful old gnarled trees at the edge of the wood. After a short distance emerge at a T-junction and a much busier road next to **The Boot** pub, where there is a bus stop with services to Ipswich and Shotley.

Cross the road carefully and turn right and then, almost immediately after the brick wall with the post box, turn left into a cul-de-sac and follow the narrow path that squeezes between the houses next to a yew hedge. This emerges at a wooded area at the bottom of gardens. Follow the path along the edge of a woodland area with a field to the right. Reaching a road, turn right and continue along a farm track as it turns to the left towards farm buildings ahead. When the track turns right towards the buildings at **Home Farm**, continue straight ahead across a large field with a hedge to the left. Cross the road and head down a track past the entrance to Woolverstone House on the right to reach open fields with the houses of the estate village of **Woolverstone** to the right and the Orwell estuary clearly visible across the fields to the left. Cross the road, where a sign to the left announces 'Woolverstone Marina', to head for Woolverstone's St Michael Church, and skirt around this to the left to follow a track that leads northeast through woodland. ◀

The church has some fancy topiary yews in its churchyard that are worth a brief look before continuing.

Follow the path past mature oaks; off to the right are modern buildings belonging to Woolverstone Hall that is now home to Ipswich Girls School. At the fence around the **marina**, turn left and then right to pass the yacht-club building, and then right again in front of its lawn to reach a jetty that has good views back along the estuary. The path continues east alongside a hedgerow before meandering slightly between woodland and the water's edge – the path can be a little muddy after rain here and also indistinct in places. Continue east along the edge of a field and soon the boats of Pin Mill come into view. Cross a footbridge and another field to follow a shady path that leads to a narrow road. Turn left and follow the road around to the right to arrive at the boatyard and the **Butt & Oyster** pub. Chelmondiston village, with pub, shop and bus connections to Ipswich and Shotley, lies just ½ mile (800m) away inland to the south.

> The riverside hamlet of **Pin Mill** is centred on sailing activities, with a sailing club and an active boatyard. In the 19th century, barges were unloaded here of goods bound for Chelmondiston and beyond. Pin Mill features in two of Arthur Ransome's children's books and was also once the repair centre for Thames barges. As well as sailing, many locals are drawn on weekends to its waterside pub that is situated in a charming, peaceful location within easy access of Ipswich.

STAGE 4
Pin Mill to Lower Holbrook

Start	Pin Mill, near Chelmondiston (TM 206 380)
Finish	Wharf near Lower Holbrook (TM 175 348)
Distance	11½ miles (18.5km)
Time	4½–5½hrs
Maps	OS Landranger 169; OS Explorer 197
Accommodation	Ipswich (hotels, guesthouses); Shotley (B&B); Harkstead (B&B)
Refreshments	Pubs at Pin Mill, Chelmondiston, Shotley Gate, Shotley and Harkstead
Public transport	Chelmondiston and Lower Holbrook both have bus services to Ipswich and Shotley.
Note	This is quite a lengthy section that some walkers might prefer to break into two stages. Shotley Gate, with its pub, facilities and bus service, serves as an ideal mid-way point.

This stretch of the Stour and Orwell Walk around the end of the Shotley peninsula, although quite long, is perhaps the most enjoyable of the entire walk. The leg between Pin Mill and Shotley Gate, alongside Shotley Marshes, is sheer delight – extremely quiet and tranquil despite the looming presence of The Port of Felixstowe across the water. The section between Shotley Gate and Lower Holbrook is mostly across open farmland, but offers some excellent views across the River Stour estuary to Essex beyond. Unfortunately, the riverside path shown along this stretch on older OS maps is no longer viable because of erosion. Nevertheless, this replacement inland route has its own rewards.

Starting at the Butt & Oyster pub at **Pin Mill**, walk a little way inland along the road past the car park and take the track that leads up steps to the left. Continue ahead between the bungalows, and follow the track that leads left along the bottom of gardens with a paddock on the right. Go through a gate to meet a 'National Trust Pin Mill' sign and take the track ahead through woodland, with moored boats visible through the trees to the left below. On meeting a track leading off to the right, continue straight on through more woodland, with plenty of nest boxes, to drop down slightly to a wooden farm building. Continue in the same direction past a footpath to the

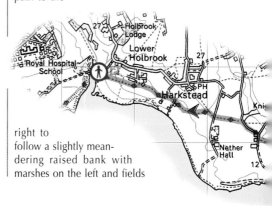

right to
follow a slightly mean-
dering raised bank with
marshes on the left and fields

on the right. Crossing a sluice, the path soon reaches an open marshy area before passing another footpath off to the right along a hedgerow.

Continue on to cross a small bridge over a stream and join a short section of boardwalk above boggy ground. The path swings around to the right towards a house. Levington church is now clearly visible across the river, as is the nearby marina. Pass a boathouse and an isolated and idyllically situated house up to the right to continue along a raised bank, with saltmarshes to the left and a dyke and fields to the right. Eventually meet steps that lead down the bank to the right at

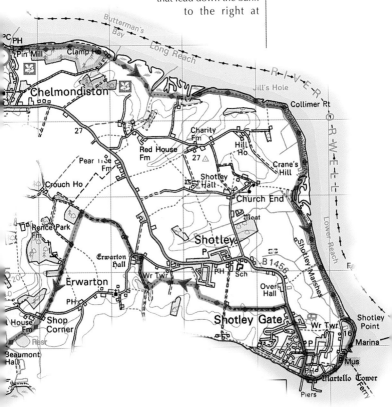

Chelmondiston Sluice North. Continue straight ahead past another footpath off to the right to reach **Collimer Point**, where the bank and track swing sharply to the right in a southerly direction. Here the Harwich skyline becomes visible in the distance, as do the cranes of The Port of Felixstowe across the water.

Continue south past the low rise of **Crane's Hill**. The path curves around a large area of marsh and meets another footpath coming in from the right. This path leads towards Shotley's St Mary's Church, a diversion of just over 1 mile (1.6km) there and back.

Shotley's **St Mary's Church**, overlooking the Orwell estuary, has hundreds of military graves from World War I, mostly Royal Navy. It also includes graves of German sailors and the victims of a collision between two submarines.

Remain on the path heading south past Shotley Marshes, enjoying the juxtaposition of peaceful, bird-filled saltmarsh of the Orwell's south bank and the

The Orwell estuary, just east of Pin Mill

frantic activity of the container port across the river. Oddly enough, from this perspective it is actually easier to make sense of the mechanics of container shipping than it is close to the mayhem on the other bank. Continue past weathered wooden groynes stretching out into the water to reach a large black-and-white painted post.

Shotley Marshes, an area of low-lying farmland behind the riverwall, is alive with flocks of Brent geese during winter. It is rich with breeding waders such as snipe, redshank and lapwing during the summer months.

A little further on, **Shotley Point** and its marina are reached, where a footpath leads right towards a Martello tower. Follow the path to the left along the seawall, keeping the **marina** to your right. Walk past a number of benches to reach a footbridge across the lock gate. Continue along the seawall, with the boatyard to the right, to arrive at the gates. ▶ Pass the **museum** and walk along King Edward VII Drive to pass two piers before arriving at the **Bristol Arms pub** and bus park.

This is close to the point where ferry passengers from Landguard Fort (Stage 1) disembark to join the route.

Shotley Gate, at the far end of the peninsula, across the water from Harwich in Essex, began life as an Anglo-Saxon settlement. An early naval battle took place here in AD885, when King Alfred of Wessex fought off invading Danes under the command of Guthrum.

Turn right and walk up the hill from the Bristol Arms, passing the post office to follow the road around to the left. Reaching the edge of the village, with fields to the right and clear views across the Orwell estuary, take the farm track to the left after the end of the appropriately named East View Terrace. This climbs gently to give views over the Stour estuary ahead. Follow the hedgerow and power lines along the edge of a very large open field. The track veers slightly to the right to pass Shotley Cottage.

Ignoring the track to the right that goes to Shotley, continue straight ahead on a footpath between fields, then turn right towards houses along another hedgerow

An avenue of sweet chestnut trees near Shotley

for a short distance before going left again across a field, parallel to the houses on the right. Cross another track and continue ahead and slightly diagonally to the right across the field to meet a fence, with a waymarked footpath leading to the left. This drops down slightly past a paddock and some conifers to reach a huge old tree, where the path continues to the right past a reservoir. Go through a gate and along an avenue of large gnarled sweet chestnut trees, past the walled farmyard and modern buildings of Erwarton Hall Farm to reach a road. Turn left along the road to pass in front of the Tudor Erwarton Hall and its very ornate pinnacle gatehouse.

Erwarton Hall, built in the 16th century, is probably most famous for its striking red-brick gatehouse. Erwarton's St Mary's Church is believed to be where Anne Boleyn's heart was buried, according to her wish, after her execution (her uncle was Sir Philip Parker of Erwarton Hall). To give some credence to this story, in 1838 a lead heart-shaped casket was discovered in an alcove of the church. It was reburied beneath the organ. The village pub, The Erwarton Queen's Head, bears a portrait of Anne Boleyn.

On the right are two minor roads. Take the second, Warren Lane, with a small pond on the corner, and follow this past Pond Farm House. The road bends left a little and crosses a track to reach a block of woodland called New Covert. Turn left alongside the wood and continue across the field at the edge of the wood towards the hedgerow ahead. Go through the gap in the hedge and continue in the same direction along a farm track between fields to reach Warren Bottom Cottages on the corner of a minor road. Follow the road in the same southerly direction past another plantation to arrive at the corner of a road and, a little further on, **Shop Corner** (although there is no shop!).

Erwarton Hall's unusual 17th-century brick gatehouse

Where the road turns sharply right take the way-marked footpath straight ahead along a hedgerow, first on the right-hand side and then on the left. Across the field to the right is Hill House Farm and, straight ahead, Beaumont Hall. Follow the path around the right-hand side of the **reservoir** and then drop down to the right towards the corner of the next field below. Go over the stile to cross the field – boggy in places – close to the fence on the right and heading towards a small footbridge ahead. Go through the gate and head across the field towards the right-hand side of the farm buildings ahead.

On reaching **Beaumont Hall Farm**, cross the farm track to traverse two large fields towards a hedgerow and a group of houses ahead. At the road, turn right then left at Needle Corner by the cottages, where there is a signpost for Harkstead. After walking for less than 5mins a footpath leads off to the left opposite a wood called Boleyn's Covert (with, perhaps, another Anne Boleyn connection). Take this across fields until reaching a minor road. Cross the road and follow the footpath slightly diagonally across the next field for a short distance before taking another footpath at the adjoining field that leads off to the left (should you wish to visit Harkstead village simply carry on towards the houses).

Harkstead is an attractive, spread-out village close to the Stour estuary that was recorded in the Domesday Book as 'Herchesteda'. The interior of the village's St Mary's Church was comprehensively refurbished in the Victorian period. Arthur Ransome was a one-time resident of Harkstead Hall.

There are very clear views across the Stour estuary from here, and for the first time the huge rocket-ship clock tower of The Royal Hospital School at Holbrook can be seen ahead. Follow the field edge next to the ditch towards the water, and then head diagonally across a field directly towards a house and the tower in the distance. At the house follow the road behind it past a private road until shortly reaching a footpath sign to the left along another minor road. Turn left and then take the next footpath to the right across a field to the corner of a hedgerow, where a fingerpost instructs you to continue alongside the hedgerow in the same direction.

The next short section of the route around Alton Green Farm is a little complicated but easy enough to follow on the ground. After passing a house and garden, the path bears right through the fence to lead through a shady copse before emerging at a bench on a green and a road. Turn left at the road to rejoin the original footpath at a gate at the edge of a field. Turn right to continue in the same direction (west) as before. Pass The Hermitage and continue along the footpath to arrive at Alton Wharf. Turn right to reach the corner of the wharf inlet. If you wish to divert from the Stour and Orwell Walk here, it is just a short distance along the road to reach a car park and **Lower Holbrook**.

STAGE 5
Lower Holbrook to Cattawade

Start	Wharf near Lower Holbrook (TM 175 348)
Finish	Cattawade picnic site (TM 101 331)
Distance	7 miles (11km)
Time	3–3½hrs
Maps	OS Landranger 169; OS Explorer 197
Accommodation	Ipswich (hotels, guesthouses)
Refreshments	Pubs at Harkstead, Stutton and Cattawade
Public transport	Lower Holbrook has bus services to Ipswich and Shotley. Cattawade has a bus service to Ipswich. Nearby Manningtree has a regular fast rail service to Ipswich and London.
Note	Just before Stutton Ness the path diverts to the beach, and this section may be impassable for short periods at high tide.

This final stage of the Stour and Orwell Walk takes in some charmingly varied countryside, with sections through farmland, quiet village lanes and along the Stour estuary itself. The first part of the walk is dominated by the presence of the vertiginous spire of the Royal Hospital School's lofty clock tower. The end of the route is at Cattawade, close to the transport hub of Manningtree, where enthusiastic walkers might feel tempted to continue west along beautiful Dedham Vale through Constable Country to follow the Stour Valley Path along the Suffolk/Essex border.

Starting at the wall at the eastern end of Alton Wharf, just south of **Lower Holbrook**, turn right and then go around the corner to the left to follow the water's edge. Passing Holbrook Boathouse, continue along the track past grazing fields to the right. Ignoring two tracks off to the right, follow the footpath along the raised bank. Once around the corner at the end of the wharf it is easy to make out the line of

The Stour and Orwell path leads around Alton Wharf close to Lower Holbrook

the original riverwall that has since been breached by the water. Continuing west along the bank, the buildings and extensive grounds of the Royal Hospital School can be seen in all their glory to the right.

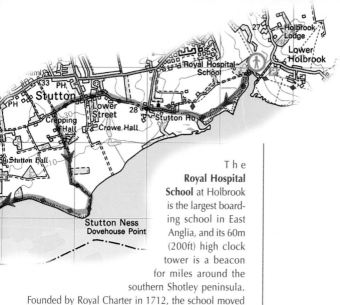

The **Royal Hospital School** at Holbrook is the largest boarding school in East Anglia, and its 60m (200ft) high clock tower is a beacon for miles around the southern Shotley peninsula. Founded by Royal Charter in 1712, the school moved from Greenwich to its present site in 1933. The school, built in neo-Georgian style and set in 200 acres, has a longstanding naval tradition that has its pupils wearing Royal Navy uniforms for ceremonial and formal events.

Soon the path along the riverwall bends to the right around another inlet. On arriving at a fence, go down the steps and across a footbridge to walk past paddocks on the left and join a footpath at the southern limit of the school's grounds. Turn left and walk parallel to the school past a couple of duck-filled ponds to continue across a grassy paddock towards the church. Arriving at the road, follow it west to pass St Peter's Church on the right.

St Peter's Church in Stutton has an interior that, although mostly Victorian in character, boasts an excellent and unusual millennium window at its west end, the work of Thomas Denny. The village once clustered around this church, but it was purposely burnt down in an attempt to stop the spread of plague. Today, most of the village lies 1.6km (1 mile) to the west.

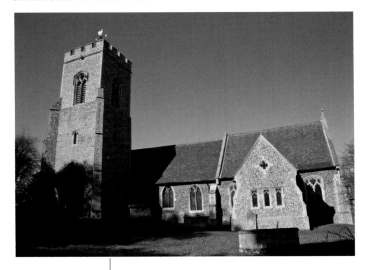

Flint-built St Peter's Church, Stutton

Walk past several attractive houses and farm buildings to pass the entrance to **Stutton House** on the left. Continue along the quiet road, with good views to the left over the River Stour and past a belt of conifers to the right. Walk through **Stutton** village, past more attractive cottages and the long, crow-steeped wall of **Crowe Hall** to the left, and past Ancient House, with some fine pargeting. At the crossroads continue in the same direction along the track past more cottages. Reaching another crossroads, turn left at a white cottage.

Pargeting (sometimes 'pargetting') is a type of decorative wall plastering that is quite commonly seen in 16th- and 17th-century buildings in parts of Suffolk. The finest local example can be seen at the Ancient House in Ipswich.

Walk south towards the estuary past a small wood and **Crepping Hall** to the left. Continue through a gate along a farm track, with views to the left of Crowe Hall. The path swings to the left to lead east for a short while, with Harwich and Felixstowe visible ahead in the distance. Turn right on reaching the water to walk along a track behind mature trees next to the shore. Just before **Stutton Ness** the path diverts to the beach, as the cliff-top path has been badly eroded.

▸ Walk east along the gravel river beach. The effects of erosion are very visible here, with many trees just hanging on with exposed roots at the cliff edge. After a little less than 1.6km (1 mile), where the beach curves inland a little around a wide bay, the footpath reverts to the cliff once more. Continue above the bridge through woodland and past a conifer belt, with a circular walk permissive footpath sign, to continue over a stile by a tennis court. Follow the path around to the right to arrive at **Stutton Mill**.

At the mill follow the path west along the river bank. From here there are open views across the Stour estuary to Manningtree in Essex ahead. At low tide the mud flats here are full of wading birds, whose piping calls may be interposed with the distant sound of the Norwich to London train line. Go over Stutton Mill Sluice, and later

This next section may be impassable for short periods of time at high tide.

Newmill Creek at Stutton Mill on the Stour estuary

another sluice, as the riverwall path curves gently around **Seafield Bay**, and the extensive maltings of Mistley are clearly visible across the water.

Reaching a hedgerow, take the path that heads inland off to the right. This leads through a gate to follow a broad, and sometimes muddy path that veers away from the riverbank alongside a reedbed to the left and a raised bank and drainage ditch and fields to the right. On arriving at a gate, take a footpath that leads sharp right up a few steps to go alongside a field. This almost immediately becomes a farm track that soon reaches a footbridge over the railway track. Cross the railway line, and then turn left along the track down that runs downhill parallel to the railway.

Mistley, across the River Stour in Essex, was once important for its sailing barges that plied between the estuary and London. The arrival of so much grain from the Suffolk hinterland made this an important centre for barley malting for beer production.

At the bottom of the hill is a sewage works on the right. Walk past this and continue to reach a large pylon, where the track swings sharply right. Follow this and, after a short distance, turn left to cross a small footbridge. Continue alongside the perimeter fence of an industrial area, with woodland and a small fishing lake just beyond to the right. The path soon skirts the lake and continues along a corridor of trees next to a field.

Emerging at a car park, walk through it to join the works road and continue straight ahead past warehouses. This soon comes out at a village street with the Crown pub opposite. Take the cul-de-sac to the left, opposite the pub, that stops just short of the busy A137. Cross the road carefully and walk down to the car park and riverside picnic area that is half-obscured by trees, just below the main road. This is **Cattawade** picnic area, the end point of the Stour and Orwell Walk and also the starting point of the Stour Valley Way.

In the early 19th century the **River Stour** was navigable as far upstream as Sudbury. Horse-drawn barges would bring bricks and grain to the estuary, where their goods would be off-loaded onto London barges at Mistley Quay. Horses were unharnessed at Brantham Lock, just above Cattawade Bridge, and barges punted under the bridge over the River Stour at Cattawade before continuing to Mistley.

Swans and decaying boat at Brantham Lock by Cattawade Bridge

THE SANDLINGS WALK
Ipswich to Southwold (59 miles/94.5km)

The lighthouse rises behind the Sole Bay Inn in Southwold town centre, at the end of the Sandlings Walk (SW, Stage 7)

STAGE 1

Ipswich to Woodbridge via Martlesham Heath

Start	Ipswich, three possible starting points – Rushmere Golf Course (TM 198 453); Heath Road (TM 196 445); St Augustine's Church (TM 195 430)
Finish	Woodbridge Tide Mill (TM 275 487)
Distance	From Rushmere Golf Course/Heath Road 8 miles (13km); from St Augustine's Church 10 miles (16km)
Time	3½–4hrs (from Rushmere Golf Course/Heath Road); 4–4½hrs (from St Augustine's Church)
Maps	OS Landranger 169; OS Explorer 197
Accommodation	Hotels and guesthouses at Ipswich and Woodbridge
Refreshments	Cafés, pubs and restaurants at Ipswich and Woodbridge
Public transport	Ipswich is well connected by rail and bus with the rest of the country. Woodbridge has regular rail connections with Ipswich and Lowestoft, and bus services to elsewhere in Suffolk.
Note	Just after Kyson Point, the route follows the bank of the Deben River north and crosses a river beach for a short distance. This might be impassable for a short period at high tide.

Unusually, this walk offers the possibility of three different starting places on the eastern side of Ipswich, with the route from St Augustine's Church being a little longer than the others. All three routes join together at Foxhall Heath to lead through Martlesham Heath and then along the west bank of the River Deben to Woodbridge.

This first leg of the Sandlings Walk is far more varied than might be imagined for one that begins in the Ipswich suburbs. Taking in urban fringe, heath, woodland, farmland and estuary, it offers a taste of many of the various landscapes and habitats that will be encountered along the length of the Sandlings Walk. A bonus is that this stage ends in the handsome town of Woodbridge, which has plenty of character and historical interest, as well as good facilities and decent transport connections.

RUSHMERE GOLF COURSE START

Starting at the entrance to Rushmere Heath (TM 198 453) on the A1214 Woodbridge road, go through the gate and follow the track diagonally across the golf course, keeping an eye out, of course, for flying golf balls. Follow the broad track that leads away from the road and, ignoring any cross-paths, keep on straight towards the concrete water tower ahead. After about ½ mile (800m), having passed a pond on the left and with the water tower away to the right, the path enters an area of woodland. Just inside the wood a waymark points the way ahead. This soon emerges at an open area, where this and the Heath Road route, that arrives from the alternative northern starting point, converge.

HEATH ROAD START

From Heath Road (TM 196 445) simply walk past the bollards at the start and take the track across the southern flank of the golf course. After just over ½ mile (800m) arrive at the point where this track converges with the path from the alternative start point at Rushmere Golf Course.

Having arrived at the point where the two northern routes converge, follow the broad track ahead, flanked by trees, with houses beyond on both sides. Reaching a road, and cross it to follow the track ahead through trees.

Follow a fence on the left and woodland on the right to pass a solitary house to the right of the track. Continue past bungalows on the left and a fenced-off Anglia Water reservoir on the right (you can see just the raised bank of this). Continue alongside the fence, ignoring any paths that veer off into the woodland to the right. Follow the

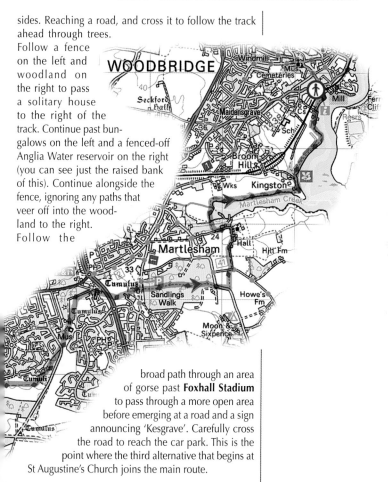

broad path through an area of gorse past **Foxhall Stadium** to pass through a more open area before emerging at a road and a sign announcing 'Kesgrave'. Carefully cross the road to reach the car park. This is the point where the third alternative that begins at St Augustine's Church joins the main route.

ST AUGUSTINE'S CHURCH START

Beginning opposite St Augustine's Church (TM 195 430) on the A1156 Bucklesham Road close to the A1189 roundabout, take the narrow track opposite the church. This leads between houses and along woodland before returning to the Bucklesham Road. Walk east along the pavement until reaching a junction to the left. Turn left and then immediately right to follow a roughly surfaced private road. This becomes an occasionally undulating dirt track as it leaves the houses and heads towards **Purdis Farm**.

Once past the farm, take the footpath left along the field edge towards the woodland to the north. Follow the sometimes muddy footpath north along the edge of woodland, sections of which are boardwalk, to reach Foxhall Road. Turn right, and after a short while take the track to the left that heads north before swinging to the right by the **stadium**. After following this for about ½ mile (800m) from its beginning at Foxhall Road, this comes out at the Kesgrave Road, just short of the village road sign. Cross the road to the car park to join the main Sandlings Walk route.

With all three routes converged, follow the broad grassy bridleway from the car park that skirts new housing development on the left, with arable fields and the radio masts of **Foxhall Heath** on the right.

A Sandlings Walk sign at Foxhall Heath, just east of Ipswich

Foxhall Radio Station was opened by the RAF in the 1940s, and later developed by the American military

during the Cold War period as part of its US military global command communications network. Should the need arise, Foxhall could provide a direct link between the Pentagon and NATO forces in Europe. The base was finally closed in 1992.

After passing a block of woodland, the area to the left is dominated by an extensive smart new housing development. The wide grassy area that the bridleway passes through is known as Long Strops.

Long Strops, a mile-long (1.6km) bridleway and public open space between Kesgrave Wood and Bell Lane, was once a track across heathland. It took its name from the old fields of 'long strops' and 'short strops' that were once located next to the track – 'strop' perhaps referring to a strip of land. Today it serves as an important green corridor for wildlife in an area of urban fringe.

Approaching a sports pitch, the Sandlings Walk path follows the fence to the right rather than the main one closer to the road and houses. At the end of the pitch it enters a wood. Bear left and then right, following the bridleway sign through the woods to reach a road, just before which is a notice board and a fenced-off grave marker – Dobb's Grave.

Dobb's Grave marks the burial place of a local shepherd, who in 1740 mislaid one of the sheep in his care and, rather than face transportation to Australia as punishment, took his own life by hanging himself in the barn at Hall Farm. In the 18th century, those who had been executed or had committed suicide were not allowed burial in the consecrated ground of a churchyard, and instead had to be buried at crossroads or at the boundaries of parishes. Today the grave is enclosed by iron railings. The unfortunate John Dobb also gave his name to the lane that passes his lonely heathland grave.

Carefully cross the road following the Sandlings Walk sign. Continue through woods to emerge at a broad track. Turn left to cross over a surfaced cycle and footpath that crosses Martlesham Heath towards the Martlesham Heath Aviation Museum. Meeting another path, turn left to follow the sign to the **museum** and walk around this, and then turn left at the concreted path. Follow this through shady wood alongside a fence. Approaching a road ahead the path swings round to the right and passes the Suffolk Constabulary headquarters just before meeting a road. Turn right and walk along the pavement on the right, with the police headquarters on the right and the busy A12 just away to the left. Follow the track that runs parallel to the A12 until reaching a track that leads left along a subway underneath the dual-carriageway. Continue ahead, with the large car park of a superstore to the right.

The path hugs the superstore perimeter fence before splitting off to the left across the gorse-covered heath. Various minor tracks join diagonally in places, but the correct one is that which remains relatively close to the southern edge of the heath. Pass close to the modern brick community hall on the right to arrive at a road with a car park on the edge of a wood opposite. Cross the road and pass the car park and picnic tables to the left to go through a gate to enter Walk Farm Wood, along what is known locally as Dr Brittain's Path.

Follow the path through the centre of the wood, passing through a large expanse of beech and an area of large oak and holly trees before reaching the road on the opposite side. Continue in the same easterly direction along the road. As the road bends round to the right at a corner, take the footpath left across a field, parallel to the east side of the wood. Go through the gap in the hedge on the other side and turn right along the road for a short distance, before turning left again on a farm track alongside a hedgerow and towards Martlesham St Mary's Church ahead. Pass a cottage before descending slightly towards the very grand **hall**. The path continues here behind the hedge that runs by the road, and bends left

by the church for about 200m before crossing the road to enter Sluice Wood.

Descending through Sluice Wood on the way to Martlesham Creek

The footpath descends steeply through Sluice Wood, carpeted with bluebells in season, along a sometimes muddy track. This emerges at a footpath along the raised bank that goes around **Martlesham Creek**, first north, then east for about 1 mile (1.6km), before reaching the confluence of the rivers Fynn and Deben.

Martlesham Creek, now a place of wading birds, respectable moorings and a boatyard, was once an important centre for the smuggling of contraband. It is reported that a one-time rector of Great Bealings, just west of Woodbridge, cooperated in this illicit trade by leaving his stables unlocked so that smugglers could avail themselves of his chaise and travel around the area without suspicion – as its owner, a man of the cloth, was naturally considered to be above suspicion.

Passing a fenced-off house to the left, turn left around the corner at Kyson Point to follow the bank of the Deben River north. It should be noted that here the Sandlings Walk crosses a river beach for a short distance that might be impassable for a short period at high tide.

Follow the surfaced path along the riverwall all the way north to Woodbridge, which by now is clearly visible ahead. There are several benches along this stretch that make a pleasant location for picnic or simply a breather. Pass Deben Yacht Club, a park area with picnic tables and Deben Rowing Club to go around an inlet where there is a footbridge over the railway line to the station. ◄ If you want to visit Woodbridge town centre, the footbridge is also a convenient means of getting there. Otherwise, continue around a quay that has a number of interesting-looking houseboats to reach a wharf where the Tide Mill lies just to the right, opposite a similarly weathered-boarded former granary that now functions as a smart restaurant.

As well as having fairly frequent trains to Ipswich and Lowestoft, the railway station at Woodbridge is also home to the well-placed Whistle Stop café.

Woodbridge Tide Mill, one of the earliest mills of this type in Britain, was originally recorded at this location in 1170, when it was operated by Augustinian monks. Henry VII took possession in 1536, at the time of the Dissolution

Tide Mill, Woodbridge, is one of only five surviving tide mills in the country

of the Monasteries, and passed it on to Queen Elizabeth I, who granted the mill to Thomas Seckford in 1564. The current wooden building dates from 1793, and is one of only five surviving tide mills in the country. It was also the last working tide mill in the UK, its wheel turning until 1957, when its oak shaft broke. The mill and granary, now a restaurant, were purchased by a private owner in 1968, and the tide mill was opened to the public in 1975 and fully refurbished in 2004.

STAGE 2
Woodbridge to Sutton Common

Start	Woodbridge Tide Mill (TM 275 487)
Finish	Sutton Common, Red Lodge (TM 334 472)
Distance	7½ miles (12km)
Time	3–3½hrs
Maps	OS Landranger 169, 156; OS Explorer 212
Accommodation	Woodbridge (hotels, guesthouses)
Refreshments	Woodbridge (pubs, cafés); Melton (pub); Wilford Bridge (pub)
Public transport	Woodbridge has regular rail connections with Ipswich and Lowestoft, and bus services to elsewhere in Suffolk. Sutton Common has no public transport connections, but Sutton village, 2 miles (3.2km) southwest of the finishing point, has a bus service to Melton and Woodbridge.

This stage of the Sandlings Walk marks a transition point of landscapes, where estuary and river give way to heath and woodland. This walk, which also takes in the attractive village of Bromeswell, begins in Woodbridge, a town worthy of exploration in its own right. As there is no accommodation at the end of this or the next stage, it makes sense for end-to-end walkers to base themselves at Woodbridge and make use of public transport to return there at the end of each day.

Starting just west of **Woodbridge Tide Mill**, take the narrow footpath between buildings that continues parallel to the railway line. This passes a marina on the right before dropping down past gardens alongside a fence and then past a boatyard. The path briefly turns left towards the railway line before turning right to run alongside it. Walk along the riverwall past a collection of maltings buildings on the other side of the tracks. Continue past more houseboats towards another marina ahead over a couple of sluices.

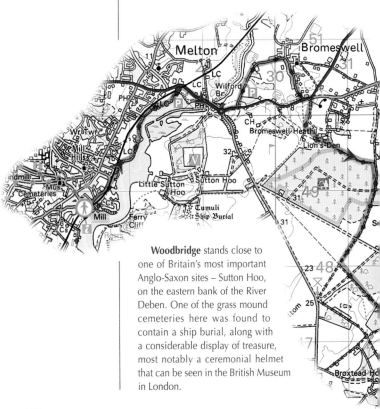

Woodbridge stands close to one of Britain's most important Anglo-Saxon sites – Sutton Hoo, on the eastern bank of the River Deben. One of the grass mound cemeteries here was found to contain a ship burial, along with a considerable display of treasure, most notably a ceremonial helmet that can be seen in the British Museum in London.

Woodbridge town, once an important centre for boat-building and rope and sail manufacture, was voted one of the UKs top six 'foodie towns' by *Country Living* magazine in 2010. The town is also home to a museum in its shire hall dedicated to the Suffolk Punch, formerly the heavy working horse of this region.

The path leads north through Melton Marina and past boatyards before curving inland around a small bay. ▶ The path continues next to the water and curves left to reach **Wilford Bridge**, with a white house on the opposite bank.

On reaching the main road crossing the bridge, where a pub bearing the same name is just a short walk to the left, turn right over the bridge. Once across, take the path left from the lay-by on the left-hand side that leads parallel to the

Exmoor ponies grazing at Sutton Common as part of a heathland management project

Just off to the left, visible through trees and connected by footpath, is Melton railway station on the Ipswich to Lowestoft line.

129

river. Continue down steps along a boardwalk next to a large area of reed marsh on the left and woods to the right. Continue over a footbridge, and follow the path up to a minor road. Turn left to follow the road up to **Bromeswell** village. The road swings around to the right and climbs gently up to the church and a road junction. Turn right past the church to descend downhill past an interesting Gothic-looking house on the right. Just before the main road is a Bromeswell village sign and the village hall.

Cross the road carefully and turn left and then, almost immediately, opposite the road junction to Snape, turn right to follow a broad sandy track that runs alongside a pine plantation. This climbs gently and, after dipping downhill again and swinging to the left, goes through a gateway to the right to cross Woodbridge Golf Course. On reaching a cross-track at one of the greens, take the path to the left towards a small white building and continue along the signed bridleway alongside an area of woodland to the left. Pass another green on the right to join a shady path that emerges at another green and a fence and a gate. Go through the gate and turn right before the path bears left again in an easterly direction along the edge of a dense pine plantation.

The track follows a fence and paddocks to the left, and after about ½ mile (800m) reaches a track at the corner of the plantation. Turn right, keeping the trees on the right and arable fields and a hedge on the left. Arriving at a crossroads of tracks, continue ahead to reach the western edge of Woodbridge Airfield, which is enclosed by tall, chain-link fencing.

Woodbridge Airfield, usually referred to as RAF Woodbridge, was originally constructed to assist damaged airplanes to land safely on long runways after raids over Germany during World War II. During the Cold War, between 1951 and 1993, it was used by USAF fighter squadrons in tandem with the nearby RAF Bentwaters. Since 2006 the base has been referred to as MoD Woodbridge, and it now serves as home to an engineer regiment of the British Army. The base's most famous association is probably with the Rendlesham Forest Incident of 1980, when US air personnel claim to have witnessed a UFO in the surrounding forest (see Stage 3, below).

Continue along the track to cross a minor, but often busy road to take the sandy track. After about 5mins turn left and southeast along the bridleway that leads alongside **Sutton Common**. At first this passes through birch woodland and heath, then, after crossing another track, runs through open heath, large fields and pine plantations. At the next crossing of tracks continue in the same direction, past sewage works on the right, and continue for a little more than ½ mile (800m) until reaching another crossroads of tracks. Turn left and walk northwest to reach the road after about 15mins, passing a thatched cottage on the right just before reaching the road. Just along the road to the right, in the trees opposite at the edge of Rendlesham Forest, is Upper Hollesley Common picnic site, while back along the road to the left, about 1½ miles (2.4km) away, is

Approaching Rendlesham Forest from Sutton Common

Sutton Common picnic site. The bunkers of Woodbridge Airfield are clearly seen stretching away to the north behind chain-link fencing.

> **Sutton Common** is one of several Sandlings locations for that elusive bird the nightjar. These hawk-like summer visitors are most commonly seen at dusk in summer – or, more likely, heard, as they have a distinctive and slightly spooky churring song that, once heard, is rarely forgotten. With a mythical ability to steal milk from goats – another name for them is 'goatsucker' – the birds have something of a supernatural character, a quality that is reinforced by their silent flight and heavily camouflaged plumage.

STAGE 3
Sutton Common to Butley via Rendlesham Forest

Start	Sutton Common, Red Lodge (TM 334 472)
Finish	Wantisden Corner, near Butley (TM 367 515)
Distance	7½ miles (12km)
Time	3–3½hrs
Maps	OS Landranger 169, 156; OS Explorer 212
Accommodation	Woodbridge (hotels, guesthouses)
Refreshments	Pubs at Shottisham and Butley
Public transport	There are buses from Butley and Shottisham to Woodbridge and Melton.

This stage of the Sandlings Walk is dominated by forest, in particular the large expanse of mostly conifers that is Rendlesham Forest. Former airfields feature prominently too. Public transport connections are few and far between at either end of this walk, and energetic walkers might want to combine this stage with the previous one, starting from Woodbridge (or perhaps Melton, which shortens the walk by 2 miles) and returning there at the end of the day. Accommodation is scarce too, so a base in Woodbridge makes sense for end-to-end walkers.

Start at **Sutton Common** (TM 334 472) on the minor road that runs along the southern edge of Rendlesham Forest. Take the trail into the forest opposite **Red Lodge**. The trail passes a car park and Upper Hollesley picnic

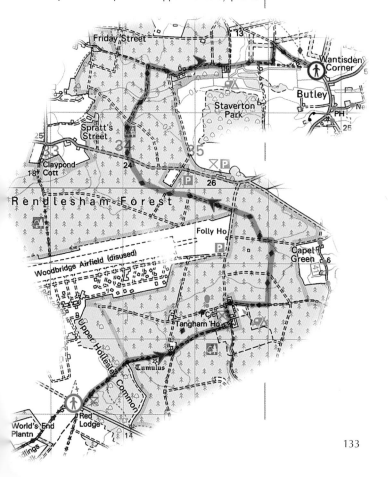

site. Go through a gate and take the track ahead past **Upper Hollesley Common** on the left, with the bunkers of MoD Woodbridge beyond. On reaching forest proper, and leaving the more open heath behind, the track twists to the right in a more easterly direction and continues straight on over a crossroads of tracks.

Continue to follow Sandlings Walk waymark posts past numerous plantations to eventually pass an isolated house on the left. A metalled road leads in the same direction towards Rendlesham Forest Centre. Follow this, then after less than ½ mile (800m) take the broad track with a 'No horse riding' sign that leads left through trees and passes several circular walk signs. After passing through an area of beeches with scattered benches, follow the waymark to the right towards the car park, now visible through the trees, to soon reach **Rendlesham Forest Walks** centre, with its toilet block, picnic area, snack and ice cream hut, information booth, a board showing the Rendlesham UFO Trail and a car park. ◄

There is also a sessile oak planted by weatherman Michael Fish in 1997 to commemorate the tenth anniversary of the 1987 Great Storm (that he famously failed to predict).

The track to East Gate, Rendlesham Forest

UFO Trail notice board at the Rendlesham Forest Walks centre

Rendlesham Forest is best known for the so-called **Rendlesham Forest Incident** of late December 1980, when a series of sightings of unexplained lights – and the alleged landing of a UFO – took place close to RAF Woodbridge, which was used at the time by the US Air Force. Apparently witnessed by a number of USAF personnel, and occasionally referred to as 'the UK Roswell', this went down in history as perhaps the most famous of Britain's UFO events. Although the MoD denied that there was ever a threat to national security, there are conspiracy theorists who claim that the incident was covered up and information suppressed.

The 'incident' began in the early morning of 26 December, when strange lights were seen through the trees near the East Gate at RAF Woodbridge. One serviceman reported encountering a flying saucer-like craft of unknown origin in the forest, which quickly disappeared, apparently leaving an impression and scorch marks.

On 28 December servicemen returning to the site claimed to see more flashing lights to the east and bright star-like lights in the sky. Despite credible explanations that the light may have been that of Orford lighthouse – or perhaps meteors, or an elaborate hoax – the legend of an extraterrestrial visit to Suffolk lives on. The Forestry Commission have responded by marking a UFO trail for walkers, which includes all the principal locations of the event.

Take the road east of the car park past the information hut and the coach parking bay. Go past a house on the left and, as the road twists to the right, continue straight ahead, heading east through a gate to walk along a broad green swathe parallel to the campsite on the right. At a crossroads of tracks, after a walk of about 5mins from the campsite, turn left through a dense pine plantation. Continue over the next crossroads of tracks and then cross a much wider track, where a UFO trail waymark points left.

Continue north to reach a T-junction, where a UFO trail heads right and the Sandlings Walk continues left. This track heads towards RAF Woodbridge East Gate (where the UFO was allegedly spotted). Follow this west for a short way before turning right again through birches and pine to reach another crossroads of tracks. Take the broad track left, which soon leads to a road and the corner of the airfield.

Cross the road and take the broad track opposite, then follow the waymark posts west to pass a Sandlings Walk sculpture, one of several along the length of the walk. After about ½ mile (800m) take the waymarked track to the right through pines and bracken to reach a

Curious sheep grazing near Wantisden Corner

road (B1084). Go straight across to follow a track north through bracken and gorse through the northern fringe of Rendlesham Forest. Cross a crossroads of tracks to continue on a gravel track through mixed woodland and over a rather sluggish stream.

Turn right at the next T-junction to follow a broad track east. This drops slightly before climbing up gently past an isolated pair of cottages and the perimeter fence of the former Bentwaters Airfield to the left. Head past the entrance to **Staverton Camping Park**, and at the next corner take the bridleway left along the edge of a field. Pass a pond to the right and the edge of a field, where the path enlarges to become a farm track.

Reaching a road with Wantisden Hall straight ahead, turn sharp right along the minor road to reach a large modern barn on the right. (Here a footpath, which may well be indistinct, leads due north up across the field to the left. This is the continuation of the Sandlings Walk.) At the barn continue along the road for a short distance to reach **Wantisden Corner** (TM 367 515). **Butley** village, with its pub and bus service, is just a 5min walk to the south.

STAGE 4

Butley to Snape Maltings via Tunstall Forest

Start	Wantisden Corner, near Butley (TM 367 515)
Finish	Snape Maltings (TM 392 574)
Distance	8 miles (13km)
Time	3–3½hrs
Maps	OS Landranger 156; OS Explorer 212
Accommodation	Hotels and guesthouses in Woodbridge and Aldeburgh
Refreshments	Butley (pub); Chillesford (pub); Snape Maltings (pub, cafés, restaurants)
Public transport	Snape Maltings has bus services from both Ipswich and Aldeburgh. Butley has a bus service to Woodbridge and Melton.

Like the stage before it, disused airfields and large tracts of forest characterise this stretch of the Sandlings Walk. The isolated church at Wantishead is well worth a short stop, and church enthusiasts might also want to detour slightly to Chillesford's St Peter's Church in order to tick off both of the only Coralline crag-towered churches in the country. Coralline crag is found only in Suffolk, and so its use as a building material is a fitting expression of the local vernacular tradition. Woodbridge and Aldeburgh, both with bus connections from Snape Maltings, make suitable bases for accommodation.

From **Wantisden Corner**, just north of Butley, take the left fork and then the right fork to reach a large modern barn on the left of the road. Across the road from here, a (probably indistinct) footpath heads due north up across the sloping field. Take this to head towards the gap in the trees on the opposite side. At the tree belt at the top of the field, continue in the same direction across the next field towards the water tower. On reaching a road with Wantisden Hall and an attractive thatched barn away to the left, continue in the same direction along a farm track towards the water tower and a church beyond. The track passes left of the **water tower** and past a large pond on the right. To the left is the perimeter fence of Bentwaters Parks, now an industrial complex but formerly and RAF airfield.

Bentwaters Parks, formerly RAF Bentwaters, was constructed in 1942 as an RAF Bomber Command base, but later transferred to Fighter Command. As part of the Twin Bases, with Woodbridge it was used by the USAF from 1951 onwards until 1993, when it was handed back to the RAF and the facility closed. According to a local paper it is said that at one time the USAF stocked enough nuclear warheads here to destroy the world several times over. As Bentwater Parks, the former airfield is now home to an enterprise park, the Bentwaters Cold War Museum, opened in 2007, and has been used frequently for television shows such as Top Gear.

Follow the track along the edge of a field to reach the small, remote Church of St John the Baptist. From here continue north along a quiet metalled road that soon bends sharply round to the right to reach a minor road after about ½ mile (800m).

The **Church of St John the Baptist** in Wantisden parish, right next to the former RAF Bentwaters base, is unusual not just for its isolation

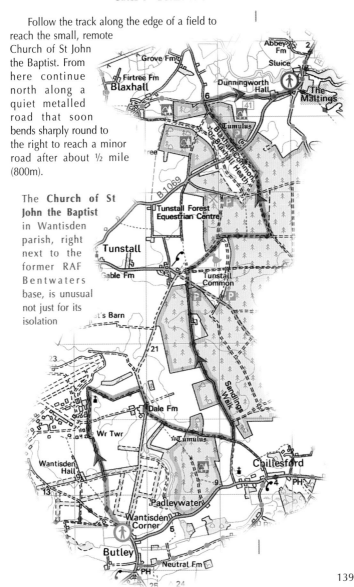

139

The Church of St John the Baptist, Wantisden, is one of just two crag-built towers in the country

but also because there never was a village here. Two isolated cottages – Bent Waters Cottages – used to exist north of the church, but these were destroyed to make way for the airfield during World War II. The church actually came within the confines of the military base until the 1950s, when a new perimeter fence placed it just outside the base, although access was impossible without a military escort until the 1960s, when a new road was built. This Norman church has a 15th-century tower built of Suffolk Coralline Crag, one of only two in the country (the other is St Peter's in neighbouring Chillesford). Guarding the south doorway is a pair of grotesque heads, and inside is an early medieval font. The cracks seen in the walls remain as evidence of a tank school accident in the 1940s.

Turn right along the road to pass the modern farm buildings at **Dale Farm**, and take the farm track along a hedgerow at the edge of a field to the left immediately after this. The track dips down, then up past a pine plantation and through a wood to reach a crossroads of tracks. Turn sharp left here towards Tunstall Forest (unless wishing to divert into Chillesford, ½ mile (800m) ahead).

Tunstall Forest was planted in the 1920s on what would have been Sandlings heath. It consists mostly of conifers, with some broadleaved belts and areas of heathland. After severe damage caused by the Great Storm of 1987, the opportunity was taken to replant the forest with a more diverse range of tree species. Star bird species here are woodlarks and nightjars. It is also a popular location for mountain biking.

Follow the track north through the edge of the forest to eventually reach a cleared area with a house before arriving at a road. Take the track straight across the road, bearing right across **Tunstall Common** to re-enter the forest, first heading east and then north, where another forest track crosses diagonally. Look carefully for waymark signs as these might be obscured by vegetation. The track eventually emerges at an open area of **Blaxhall Heath**, where it crosses a road (**B1069**) by a car park

Mushrooms growing by the wayside in Tunstall Forest

before continuing across the heath alongside the edge of woodland.

The track across the heath merges into a more substantial road to join a minor road at a crossroads. Turn right to follow the road to reach the junction with the B1069 next to **Dunningworth Hall**. Turn left, being careful of motor traffic, to soon reach **Snape Maltings**.

STAGE 5
Snape Maltings to Thorpeness

Start	Snape Maltings (TM 392 574)
Finish	West of Thorpeness on B1353 (TM 462 604)
Distance	7½ miles (12km)
Time	3–3½hrs
Maps	OS Landranger 156; OS Explorer 212
Accommodation	Thorpeness (hotel and self-catering)
Refreshments	Snape Maltings (pub, cafés, restaurants); Snape (pub); Friston (pub); Thorpeness (pub)
Public transport	Thorpeness has four buses a day (Nightingales of Beccles 521 service) to and from Halesworth via Darsham and Saxmundham, all of which have rail stations on the East Suffolk Line. Thorpeness also has morning buses to Ipswich on schooldays, and links to Rendlesham and Wickham Market (with connections to Ipswich) using the Coastal Accessible Transport Service (www.cats-paws.co.uk) that must be booked the day before (01728 833526). Aldeburgh, just south of Thorpeness, has a regular bus service to Woodbridge and Ipswich. Snape Maltings has a bus service from both Ipswich and Aldeburgh.

In contrast to the three preceding stages, this section of the Sandlings Walk offers a splendid array of creature comforts at either end, at Snape Maltings and at Thorpeness, both of which have all the trappings of civilisation

– cafés, pubs, gift shops and ample car parking. Both have fairly reasonable public transport connections too. En route, this stage passes through open farmland, isolated patches of woodland and an RSPB reserve with typical Sandlings habitat.

Starting at **Snape Maltings**, head north across the bridge over the River Alde and follow the footpath on the left-hand side of the busy road into Snape village.

The small village of **Snape** has an interesting village sign that gives several clues to its history. The Anglo-Saxon ship depicted in the top left quarter refers to the Saxon burial grounds found nearby, while the praying monk is a reference to the Benedictine order formerly at the Priory of St Mary, the remains of which lie under the Chapel Fields. The bridge shown lower left depicts the beautiful old bridge that was demolished in the 1960s to make room for a more car-friendly one, while the curlew, lower right, is a nod to Benjamin Britten, who lived locally and drew inspiration from the area.

A Virginia creeper-covered building at Snape Maltings

The village sign at Snape gives an account of the village's history

The wrought-iron cross above the sign is based on the Consecration Cross found inside the village's 13th-century Church of St John the Baptist, and the supports beneath the sign symbolise the reeds that grow by the River Alde.

In the village, just beyond the Crown Inn, on the right, is a crossroads, where you turn right. Pass another pub on the left, the Golden Key, and continue along the road to reach the edge of the village. At the junction, do not head along the bridleway, but continue along the road past the tall farm buildings of the appropriately named **Rookery Farm**.

The road narrows and, after passing a footpath to the left that leads to a church and **The Priory** to the right, joins the A1094, a considerably busier road, at a T-junction. Cross carefully to go along a track past a bungalow and a footpath crossroads to continue north towards some pylons. Follow the hedgerow and the telephone wires along the byway until reaching a farm track sharply off to the right that leads to a group of farm buildings ahead. Follow this, keeping to the footpath to pass the walls of **Friston Hall** on your left.

Look for a gap in the hedge to the right before reaching the large stump of a horse chestnut tree. Go through the gap and walk across two fields directly towards the windmill. The white dome of Sizewell B power station also becomes visible here for the first time on this route. Reaching the road, turn left past cottages to arrive at a junction. Cross over and walk along Grove Road past more cottages until reaching a footpath to the right, where the road swings to the left. Take the footpath diagonally across the field to join up with a lane at the corner of the field. Turn right to follow the lane east.

map continues on page 146

Friston Windmill, a grade II listed post mill, was erected by the Melton millwright in 1812. A pair of sails was removed in 1943, but the mill continued to operate with just two until 1956,

145

Wheat fields and big skies near Friston in high summer

when wind power was replaced by a diesel engine. Permission was given to demolish it in 1965, but fortunately this did not take place, and it was later agreed that it should be moved to the Museum of East Anglian Life at Stowmarket. However, in 1972 its new owner decided to preserve it, and the mill was fully restored.

The lane curves south, close to a patch of woodland parallel to electricity pylons that lead

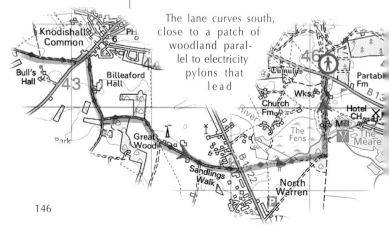

to Sizewell power station. Go past a bridleway to the left and alongside an open area known as **Knodishall Common**. The track drops down slightly before reaching a road with a speed limit sign. Turn left along the road past a line of bungalows to walk a little way before taking the first road to the right. The road soon downgrades from tarmac to concrete and passes **Billeaford Hall** to reach a junction to the left at the edge of a large wooded area marked on maps as **Great Wood**.

Turn left, taking the bridleway heading left alongside the edge of the wood. This shady track follows a coppiced hazel hedge towards a large radio pylon ahead. The track swings around the edge of a field to turn directly towards the **radio mast**, where there is a bridleway sign that points straight on for the Sandlings Walk. Go through a gap in the hedge next to some buildings and an electricity relay station. The track continues past farm buildings and a private road to the right before dropping down slightly past more buildings to meet the main Leiston to Aldeburgh road, the **B1122**. Cross the road and take the path opposite through North Warren conservation area.

North Warren RSPB reserve combines an extensive area of Sandlings heath with a mixture of reedbed, shingle, dune and woodland habitat. Important conservation bird species found here include nightingale, woodlark, Dartford warbler and marsh harrier, with bitterns breeding in the reedbeds. Small numbers of red deer and muntjac are also present, along with otters, water vole, badgers and numerous rabbits. Reptiles are well represented too, with adder, slow worm and common lizard all recorded in the heath areas. Of insect species, among a wide variety of butterflies is the nationally rare silver-studded blue.

rpeness

On reaching a wooded area and a bench, continue straight ahead through an area of typical Sandlings heath before turning left on meeting a track that crosses

in another woodland area. Reaching a fence, take the path that leads left to Thorpeness along a raised bank, with woodland to the left and open marshes beyond the trees to the right. Cross a bridge over a murky mill pond and, arriving at the school, take the path to the right and then left to follow the waymark at the back of the house. Continue to reach a car park and golf course, then bear left along the track, which twists past a pond to reach the **B1353**. The Sandlings Walk continues directly opposite; **Thorpeness** is less than a 1 mile (1.6km) walk along the main road to the right.

STAGE 6
Thorpeness to Dunwich Heath

Start	West of Thorpeness on B1353 (TM 462 604)
Finish	Dunwich Heath NT visitor centre (TM 477 677)
Distance	8½ miles (13.5km)
Time	3½–4hrs
Maps	OS Landranger 156; OS Explorer 231, 212
Accommodation	Thorpeness (hotel, holiday lets); Eastbridge (pub)
Refreshments	Thorpeness (pubs, cafés); Sizewell (pub); Eastbridge (pub); Dunwich Heath NT visitor centre (café)
Public transport	Thorpeness has four buses a day to and from Halesworth via Darsham and Saxmundham, all of which have rail stations on the East Suffolk Line. Thorpeness also has morning buses to Ipswich on schooldays, and links to Rendlesham and Wickham Market (with connections to Ipswich) using the Coastal Accessible Transport Service (www.cats-paws.co.uk) that must be booked the day before (01728 833526). Aldeburgh, just south of Thorpeness, has regular bus services to Woodbridge and Ipswich. Dunwich Heath has no public transport, but Dunwich village has occasional services to Darsham and Saxmundham and connections using the Coastal Accessible Transport Service that must be pre-booked.

Beginning and ending at extensive areas of heath typical of the Sandlings landscape, this stage also takes in the only coastal stretch of the Sandlings Walk – a short section past Sizewell nuclear power station that is shared with the Suffolk Coast and Heaths Path.

Start on the B1353, just west of **Thorpeness** village, next to the golf course, where the Sandlings Walk crosses the road on a waymarked surfaced track heading north. Go past a signpost for 'Aldringham Walks' to reach a corner and follow the waymark to head right. The path widens out as it passes through an area of typical Sandlings heath. Continue past a track to the right that leads to a house and, shortly after, another footpath to the right. The path continues past fields with World War II concrete bunkers, and the dome of **Sizewell B nuclear power station** becomes increasingly predominant as the path heads north. Cross another track to continue straight ahead along a track with a high hedge to reach a track to the right that leads to the beach.

Walk north along the road next to an area of woodland belonging to **Sizewell Hall**. Go past a

map continues on page 151

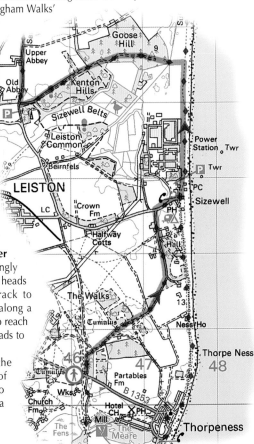

A pub sign in Sizewell village, showing three meanings of 'vulcan'

footpath to the left that leads through an area of bracken and past another signed 'Aldringham Walks'. Continue heading north towards Sizewell nuclear power station, past a farm on the left, to meet a road junction. Turn right into **Sizewell** village along the road and pass the power station visitor centre on the left opposite the Vulcan Arms, with its interesting pub sign that illustrates three different meanings of the word 'vulcan'. On reaching the beach café, continue north along the track that leads in front of the **power station**. ◄

From here, for the next mile (1.6km) or so, the Sandlings Walk follows the same route as the Suffolk Coast Path.

Looking towards the 'golf ball' of Sizewell B nuclear power station

After passing the power station, the Sandlings Walk leads inland towards Kenton Hills. It follows a broad track, left, through a large conifer plantation past Goose Hill Marshes to continue alongside **Kenton Hills**, a large stand of mixed woodland, with open fields to the right. The track climbs slightly towards a gate and continues to a T-junction, where you turn right along an unsurfaced road and head north past **Old Abbey Farm**. Pass a track over the fields to the right, and fork left where the track divides at **Potter's Farm**. Turn right at the road to walk past a track signposted to 'Lower Abbey Farm', to the right, to reach the village of **Eastbridge**, which has its own charming pub, the Eels Foot Inn.

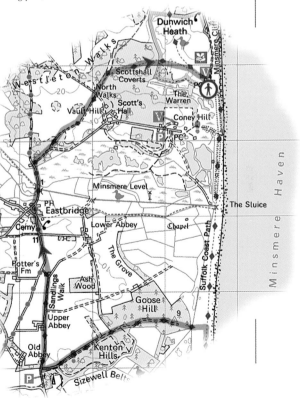

Yellow water lilies growing on the water near Eastbridge

The **Eels Foot Inn** in Eastbridge dates back to the 17th century and was once a favoured haunt of sheep drovers and smugglers. These days it is more associated with song, having informal folk sessions weekly on Thursday nights and on the last Sunday of the month. Morris dancers perform sometimes too.

Continuing north, leave the village to walk over a small bridge, and then another over a stream that has yellow water lilies covering the water in season. A little further on, a track leads off to the right through dense coppiced woodland into Minsmere RSPB reserve. After about ¼ mile (400m) a track forks off to the left. Take this to leave the wooded area and follow the track to **Vault Hill**, an open area with views across to the coast and the mushroom of Sizewell B. Arriving at a crossroads that has a track leading right towards the Minsmere RSPB reserve visitor centre, continue straight on through woodland along an avenue of oaks until reaching a waymark, where you bear right along a slightly narrower track. Reaching a gate and a sign that announces 'NT Dunwich Heath', continue straight on across the heath – a blaze of purple in August – to arrive at the coastguard cottages and the

Dunwich Heath National Trust visitor centre with its tea-room, shop, toilet facilities and car park.

> **Coppicing** is a woodland management technique that encourages new growth from tree stumps by cutting them down close to ground level at regular intervals, usually every few years. The new shoots that develop can be used for poles or firewood, and an area of woodland can be sustainably managed using this ancient practice that maintains trees at a juvenile stage more or less indefinitely. Coppicing creates a rich variety of habitats and generally encourages biodiversity, allowing woodland plants such as bluebell and anemone to thrive in the increased light that results from cutting, and scarce birds such as nightingale and nightjar to colonise the open areas. Trees that have traditionally been coppiced in Suffolk are hazel, beech, alder and willow.

STAGE 7
Dunwich Heath to Southwold

Start	Dunwich Heath NT visitor centre (TM 477 677)
Finish	Southwold, sea front (TM 510 763)
Distance	12 miles (19km)
Time	5–6hrs
Maps	OS Landranger 156; OS Explorer 212
Accommodation	Southwold (hotels, guesthouses); Walberswick (B&Bs)
Refreshments	Dunwich Heath (café); Dunwich (café, pub); Walberswick (cafés, pub); Southwold (cafés, pubs)
Public transport	Dunwich Heath has no public transport, but nearby Dunwich village has occasional services to Darsham and Saxmundham, as well as connections using the Coastal Accessible Transport Service (www.cats-paws.co.uk) that must be pre-booked. Southwold has bus services to Lowestoft, Halesworth and Norwich, which has a direct train service to London.

The last stage of the Sandlings Walk does full justice to its name, passing through archetypal Sandlings heath landscape for most of the way. By way of contrast, the gorse-filled heath walking is broken up nicely by some pleasant stretches of woodland. To cap a lovely day out, and as a fitting end to an enjoyable long-distance walk, there is also intriguing, disappearing Dunwich to savour and the old-fashioned charms – and excellent pubs and tearooms – of Southwold for a finale.

Starting at the car park at **Dunwich Heath** National Trust visitor centre take the waymarked path northwest across Dunwich Heath, retracing briefly the last stretch of the previous stage. Before long the path splits – take the right fork that follows the same route as the Suffolk Coast Path to Dunwich village. Cross the heath to reach a bridleway and a road that leads to **Mount Pleasant Farm** ahead. Turn right along the bridleway to reach a minor road after about ¼ mile (400m). Cross the road to enter the mixed woodland of **Grey Friars Wood**, and after passing a house follow a broad track through a gate and past more houses to reach a road. Turn right then take another track off to the right that leads past several attractive cottages to go through woodland that eventually emerges at a gap in ancient wall.

Follow the wall towards the sea briefly, before swinging left to continue north along the track parallel to the coast. To the left, across a field, are the ruins of Greyfriars Priory, which make for an interesting short detour. The cliff edge path continues a little further before dropping down to the left to reach **Dunwich** village at the Westleton road. Turn right and then left to pass the Ship Inn and Dunwich Museum virtually next door.

Walk down to the church, and at the road junction take the track that continues west alongside a wooded bank and a pair of cottages. It follows a green lane between hedgerows before passing through woodland to reach **Sandy Lane Farm** on the right. Just past the farm turn right where two tracks meet and continue over another cross-track. Pass another house to the left, through mixed woodland, to arrive at a notice board announcing 'Westleton Heath'.

map continues on page 156

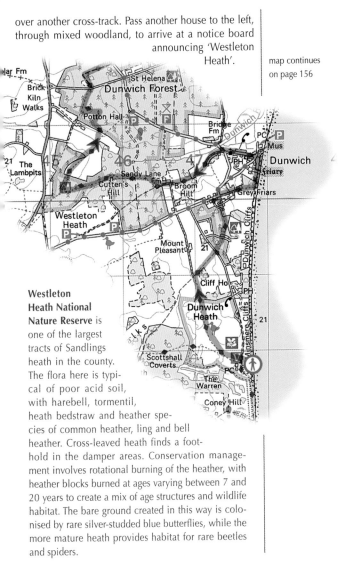

Westleton Heath National Nature Reserve is one of the largest tracts of Sandlings heath in the county. The flora here is typical of poor acid soil, with harebell, tormentil, heath bedstraw and heather species of common heather, ling and bell heather. Cross-leaved heath finds a foothold in the damper areas. Conservation management involves rotational burning of the heather, with heather blocks burned at ages varying between 7 and 20 years to create a mix of age structures and wildlife habitat. The bare ground created in this way is colonised by rare silver-studded blue butterflies, while the more mature heath provides habitat for rare beetles and spiders.

Typical Sandlings heath at Westleton Heath National Nature Reserve

Continue through birches to reach the edge of the wood. Continue through a gate in the same direction and climb gently to reach a cross-track near the top of the incline. Take the permissive path through private land that leads to the right.

Follow the narrow path that squeezes between tall gorse bushes where, on warm sunny days, the air is redolent with their almond scent. When the path reaches an open area, follow the path ahead on the right of the hedge alongside a large field. Once across the field go through the gap in the hedge and ignoring

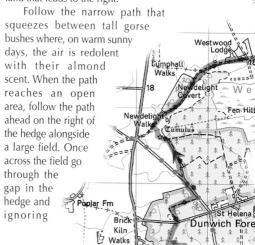

the private track to the left, continue along the public footpath over a bridge that spans a small brook. The path climbs up through gorse to reach a cross track where there is a bench that makes an ideal rest spot.

Turn left to walk along a gorse-lined path with good views to the south. Look out for a waymark at the side of the path a couple of minutes' walk beyond the bench. This is easy to miss, as it may be overgrown with gorse, but it coincides with the edge of pine plantation just to the north. Turn right across the heath towards the western end of the pine plantation. At the edge of the plantation con-tinue along a broad track through part of Dunwich Forest.

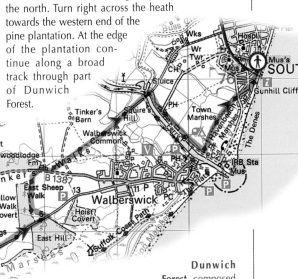

Dunwich Forest, composed of mixed coniferous and broad-leaved species, is currently undergoing a process of 'rewilding' as part of a long-term plan to recreate the natural landscape that existed before the advent of extensive conifer plantations. The northern part of the forest is managed by the Suffolk Wildlife Trust and grazed by a herd of Dartmoor ponies in order for it to develop into predominantly deciduous woodland. The RSPB manage the heathland area to the south. They hope to increase the area of lowland heath as conifers

Nightjar sculpture along Sandlings Walk at Westleton Heath

are gradually felled and areas of deciduous trees are allowed to revert to heather.

At the next track crossing take the waymarked path to the left through pines and birches and then turn right at the next T-junction that comes soon after. Head north through gorse and open heath, where there is a Sandlings Walk nightjar sculpture at the side of the path. The track continues, squeezing through gorse bushes, to reach a road. Cross over, turn right and immediately left to follow a forest track past an old quarry just off to the left. After a few minutes turn sharp right along another grassy track that leads along a shady route to reach another road.

Go straight across the road through a gate and then turn left along a path that follows a fence parallel to the road. After passing a couple of metal gates that lead back to the road, turn left along a broader track with gorse bushes that gradually swings away from the road. Reach a track by a large birch wood and turn left through a gate over a cattle grid. Pass a field to the left that has a number of noticeable **tumuli**. Go through a gate to head left towards a car park and then, almost immediately, turn back sharp right by a stone sculpture that lies in the grass island between the tracks.

Follow the broad sandy track in a north-easterly direction. This undulates through heath and patches of woodland past a few isolated cottages before climbing a little to reach, after about 1 mile (1.6km), a very grand house on the left, half-hidden behind walls and tall trees. This is **Westwood Lodge**, an opulent country house with an odd central viewing tower in its roof that must afford one of the best views in the county.

Just beyond the lodge the track turns into a metalled road as it continues in the same direction towards Walberswick. After a road walk of about 1 mile (1.6km) it passes a wood on the left called **Sallow Walk Covert**, and a little way downhill from here a bridleway leads left through a gate to lead diagonally across a meadow back towards the wood. Follow this to the wood's edge, and then head north along the side of the wood to reach its northern perimeter. Walberswick church is now clearly visible away to the right, as well as the buildings of Southwold beyond.

Approaching the **B1387**, take the waymarked footpath to the right across a field towards a farmhouse. Turn right at the road and walk past the farmhouse before immediately going left through a gate where a sign welcomes you to Walberswick National Nature Reserve. This is part of Walberswick Common known as **Tinker's Walks**. Follow the track straight ahead across the common towards Southwold's water tower in the distance.

Many of the old **sheep walks** of the Suffolk Sandlings still retain their names if not their sheep – Tinkers Walk's, East Sheep Walk, Newdelight Walks, Westleton Walks – all of these refer to places where flocks of sheep once grazed extensively. Although recorded in the Domesday Book, sheep farming in coastal Suffolk reached its peak in the 17th and 18th centuries, with a flock of 1600 sheep being recorded from Tinker's Walks in 1795. Sheep would graze on the heath by

The approach to Southwold across Walberswick Common

Alexanders and moored boats along the River Blyth, near Southwold

day, but were led to enclosures at night so that their droppings might fertilise the soil. The so-called 'walks' resulted from daily routine of leading flocks from heath to enclosure. Sheep farming largely disappeared from the Sandlings by the early 20th century, but small flocks have recently been reintroduced in places such as Sutton Heath to assist with conservation work.

After going through a gate, a track leads off right towards Walberswick church. Ignore this and continue in the same direction, climbing up a low rise to get a nice clear view of Southwold lighthouse ahead. You soon reach a smooth tarmac track, with an immense reedbed to the left that is alive with warblers' song in early summer. Beyond the reeds and across the river to the left a capped windmill can be seen, while straight ahead is the distinctive skyline of Southwold, with its church, water tower and lighthouse. Continue along the tarmac path to reach the Bailey bridge that crosses the River Blyth.

Cross the bridge to the Southwold shore and follow the path – now merged with the Suffolk Coast and Heaths Path – southeast along the north bank of the River Blyth past the **Harbour Inn**, Southwold Sailing Club, numerous boatyards and fish huts selling excellent, well-priced and very fresh produce. Just beyond the quay for the passenger ferry to Walberswick, and just before the caravan and camping site, turn left through the bank to follow the path alongside **Town Marshes**.

After about ½ mile (800m) it passes a group of benches and a concrete nightjar sculpture before coming out at a road. Cross the road and go up Constitution Hill, past cottages on the left and one of Southwold's 'greens' on the right.

Southwold's famous **'greens'** came about after the great fire of 1659, when the town authorities, in their wisdom, decided to create fire breaks as an integral part of the rebuilding programme. There are nine in total – Bartholomew Green, East Green, South Green, and so on – which, as well as their obvious fire-safety function, afford good views to many corners of the town. South Green has probably the best view of all, while St James's Green was once the home of Southwold's coastguard station and still has the rigged mast formerly used for signalling.

Reaching the Red Lion pub at the top, either turn right to the seafront or continue along a little way along Pinkney's Lane to reach the High Street in **Southwold** and the town's much lauded Swan Hotel. The choice is entirely yours – you have now completed the Sandlings Walk.

Two forms of transport along the banks of the River Blyth, near Southwold

APPENDIX A

Route summary table

The Suffolk Coast Path

Stage	Start	Finish	Distance	Time	Notes on alternative routes and ferries
1	Lowestoft	Covehithe	9 miles (14.5km) (inland route); 7 miles (11km) (beach route)	3–4hrs (inland route); 2½–3hrs (beach route)	Inland route advisable at high tide
2	Covehithe	Southwold	7 miles (11km) (inland route); 4 miles (6.5km) (coast route)	2½–3hrs (inland route); 1½–2hrs (coast route)	Inland route advisable at high tide
3	Southwold	Dunwich	6½ miles (10.5km)	2½–3hrs	Short-cut possible by Walberswick ferry (seasonal)
4	Dunwich	Thorpeness	8 miles (13km)	3–3½hrs	Alternative inland route at high tide or with dogs (May–Sept)
5	Thorpeness	Snape Maltings	6½ miles (10.5km)	2½–3hrs	
6	Snape Maltings	Chillesford	4½ miles (7.5km); via Orford Loop (to Chillesford or Butley ferry) 13½ miles (22km)	2–2½hrs; via Orford Loop (to Chillesford or Butley ferry) 5–6hrs	Alternative route: Orford Loop to Chillesford (or continuation to Butley ferry). Butley ferry is seasonal.

Stage	Start	Finish	Distance	Time	Notes on alternative routes and ferries
7	Chillesford	Shingle Street	8 miles (13km)	3–4hrs	Orford Loop continuation to Butley ferry rejoins main route on this stage
8	Shingle Street	Landguard Fort, Felixstowe	10½ miles (17km)	4–5hrs (excluding ferry waiting time)	Inland route avoids shingle beach. Main route goes via ferry (seasonal) from Bawdsey Quay to Felixstowe Ferry.

The Stour and Orwell Walk

Stage	Start	Finish	Distance	Time	Notes on alternative routes and ferries
1	Landguard Fort, Felixstowe	Nacton	10 miles (16km)	4–4½hrs	Ferry from Landguard Fort to Shotley Gate (seasonal) can be used to reach mid-point of Stage 4. Alternative route (½ mile/800m) avoids the main railway crossing in Felixstowe.
2	Nacton	Orwell Bridge, Ipswich	4 miles (6.5km) to Orwell Bridge; Ipswich Loop an extra 5–6 miles (8–9.5km)	1½–2hrs to Orwell Bridge; Ipswich Loop 2–2½hrs	Ipswich Loop avoids crossing the Orwell Bridge, Ipswich
3	Orwell Bridge, Ipswich	Pin Mill	10 miles (16km)	3½–4hrs	
4	Pin Mill	Lower Holbrook	11½ miles (18.5km)	4½–5½hrs	
5	Lower Holbrook	Cattawade	7 miles (11km)	3–3½hrs	

The Sandlings Walk

Stage	Start	Finish	Distance	Time	Notes on alternative routes and ferries
1	Ipswich	Woodbridge	8 miles (13km) (from Rushmere Golf Course/Heath Road); 10 miles (16km) (from St Augustine's Church)	3½–4hrs (from Rushmere Golf Course/Heath Road); 4–4½hrs (from St Augustine's Church)	Three possible start points
2	Woodbridge	Sutton Common	7½ miles (12km)	3–3½hrs	
3	Sutton Common	Butley	7½ miles (12km)	3–3½hrs	
4	Butley	Snape Maltings	8 miles (13km)	3–3½hrs	
5	Snape Maltings	Thorpeness	7½ miles (12km)	3–3½hrs	
6	Thorpeness	Dunwich Heath	8½ miles (13.5km)	3½–4hrs	
7	Dunwich Heath	Southwold	12 miles (19km)	5–6hrs	

APPENDIX B

Useful contacts

Suffolk Coast and Heaths AONB unit
Dock Lane
Melton
Woodbridge
Suffolk IP 1PE
Tel: 01394 384948
www.suffolkcoastandheaths.org

Choose Suffolk Tourist Partnership
Felaw Maltings
Felaw Street
Ipswich
Suffolk IP2 8SQ
Tel: 01473 406711
www.choosesuffolk.com

Discover Suffolk
Suffolk County Council
Countryside Access
8 Russell Road
Ipswich IP1 2BX
www.discoversuffolk.org.uk

The Suffolk Coast
www.thesuffolkcoast.co.uk

Visit Suffolk Coast
www.visit-suffolkcoast.co.uk

Visit Suffolk
www.visitsuffolk.com

Tide tables
www.tidetimes.org.uk

The Long Distance Walkers Association
www.ldwa.org.uk

Ramblers Association
2nd Floor, Camelford House
87–90 Albert Embankment
London SE1 7TW
Tel: 020 7339 8500
www.ramblers.org.uk

Transport operators
National Rail
Tel: 0871 200 4950
www.nationalrail.co.uk

National Express
Tel: 08717 818178
www.nationalexpress.com

East Suffolk Railway Line
www.eastsuffolkline.com

Coastal Accessible Transport Service
Tel: 01728 830516
www.cats-paws.co.uk

Traveline East Anglia
Tel: 0871 200 2233
www.travelineeastanglia.org.uk

Butley to Orford Ferry
Tel: 07913 672499

Felixstowe to Bawdsey Ferry
Tel: 07709 411511

Walberswick to Southwold Ferry
Tel: 01502 478712

Harwich Harbour Ferry
Tel: 07919 911440
www.harwichharbourferry.com

Tourist Information Centres

Aldeburgh
152 High Street
Aldeburgh
Suffolk IP15 5AQ
Tel: 01728 453637
www.suffolkcoastal.gov.uk

Felixstowe
91 Undercliff Road West
Felixstowe
Suffolk IP11 2AF
Tel: 01394 276770
www.suffolkcoastal.gov.uk

Ipswich
St Stephens Church
St Stephens Lane
Ipswich
Suffolk IP1 1DP
Tel: 01473 258070
www.ipswich.gov.uk

Lowestoft
East Point Pavilion
Royal Plain
Lowestoft
Suffolk NR33 0AP
Tel: 01502 533600
www.visit-lowestoft.co.uk

Southwold
69 High Street
Southwold
Suffolk IP18 6DS
Tel: 01502 724729
www.visit-lowestoft.co.uk

Woodbridge
The Station
Woodbridge
Suffolk IP12 4AJ
Tel: 01394 382240
www.suffolkcoastal.gov.uk

APPENDIX C
Further reading

Some of the titles listed below may be out of print, but are still worth seeking out.

A Bankes and J Reekie, *New Aldeburgh Anthology* (Boydell Press)

S Barnes, *Flying in the Face of Nature: a year in the Minsmere Bird Reserve* (Pelham Books)

D Church and A Gander, *The Story of the Southwold–Walberswick Ferry* (Holm Oak)

J Gibbs, *The Suffolk Coast* (Frances Lincoln)

P Heazell, *Most Secret: the hidden history of Orford Ness* (The History Press)

C Hegarty and S Newsome, *Suffolk's Defended Shore: coastal fortifications from the air* (English Heritage)

L Mitchell, *Slow Norfolk & Suffolk* (Bradt/Alastair Sawday's)

DP Mortlock, *The Guide to Suffolk Churches* (Lutterworth Press)

GC Munn, *Southwold: an earthly paradise* (Antique Collector's Club)

National Trust, *Dunwich Heath* (The History Press)

S O'Dell, *Essex and Suffolk Stour: a history* (The History Press)

M Page and P Young, *Suffolk Coast from the Air* (Halsgrove)

R Parker, *Men of Dunwich: the story of a vanished town* (Holt, Rinehart & Winston)

T Williamson, *Sandlands: the Suffolk coast and heaths* (Windgather Press)

NOTES

NOTES

LISTING OF CICERONE GUIDES

Tour of the Vanoise
Trekking in the Vosges and Jura
Vanoise Ski Touring
Walking in Provence
Walking in the Cathar Region
Walking in the Cevennes
Walking in the Dordogne
Walking in the Haute Savoie
North & South
Walking in the Languedoc
Walking in the Tarentaise and
Beaufortain Alps
Walking on Corsica

GERMANY

Germany's Romantic Road
Walking in the Bavarian Alps
Walking in the Harz Mountains
Walking the River Rhine Trail

HIMALAYA

Annapurna: A Trekker's Guide
Bhutan
Everest: A Trekker's Guide
Garhwal and Kumaon: A
Trekker's and Visitor's Guide
Kangchenjunga: A Trekker's
Guide
Langtang with Gosainkund and
Helambu: A Trekker's Guide
Manaslu: A Trekker's Guide
The Mount Kailash Trek

IRELAND

Irish Coastal Walks
The Irish Coast to Coast Walk
The Mountains of Ireland

ITALY

Gran Paradiso
Italy's Sibillini National Park
Shorter Walks in the Dolomites
Through the Italian Alps
Trekking in the Apennines
Trekking in the Dolomites
Via Ferratas of the Italian
Dolomites: Vols 1 & 2
Walking in Abruzzo
Walking in Sardinia
Walking in Sicily
Walking in the Central Italian
Alps
Walking in the Dolomites

Walking in Tuscany
Walking on the Amalfi Coast

MEDITERRANEAN

Jordan – Walks, Treks, Caves,
Climbs and Canyons
The Ala Dag
The High Mountains of Crete
The Mountains of Greece
Treks and Climbs in Wadi
Rum, Jordan
Walking in Malta
Western Crete

NORTH AMERICA

British Columbia
The Grand Canyon
The John Muir Trail
The Pacific Crest Trail

SOUTH AMERICA

Aconcagua and the Southern
Andes
Hiking and Biking Peru's Inca
Trails
Torres del Paine

SCANDINAVIA

Trekking in Greenland
Walking in Norway

SLOVENIA, CROATIA AND MONTENEGRO

The Julian Alps of Slovenia
The Mountains of Montenegro
Trekking in Slovenia
Walking in Croatia

SPAIN AND PORTUGAL

Costa Blanca Walks
1 West & 2 East
Mountain Walking in Southern
Catalunya
The Mountains of Central Spain
Trekking through Mallorca
Walking in Madeira
Walking in Mallorca
Walking in the Algarve
Walking in the Canary Islands
2 East
Walking in the Cordillera
Cantabrica
Walking in the Sierra Nevada

Walking on La Gomera and
El Hierro
Walking on La Palma
Walking on Tenerife
Walking the GR7 in Andalucia
Walks and Climbs in the Picos
de Europa

SWITZERLAND

Alpine Pass Route
Central Switzerland
The Bernese Alps
Tour of the Jungfrau Region
Walking in the Valais
Walking in Ticino
Walks in the Engadine

TECHNIQUES

Geocaching in the UK
Indoor Climbing
Lightweight Camping
Map and Compass
Mountain Weather
Moveable Feasts
Outdoor Photography
Rock Climbing
Sport Climbing
The Book of the Bivvy
The Hillwalker's Guide to
Mountaineering
The Hillwalker's Manual

MINI GUIDES

Avalanche!
Navigating with a GPS
Navigation
Pocket First Aid and Wilderness
Medicine
Snow

For full information on all
our guides, and to order
books and eBooks, visit our
website:
www.cicerone.co.uk.

Walking – Trekking – Mountaineering – Climbing – Cycling

Over 40 years, Cicerone have built up an outstanding collection of 300 guides, inspiring all sorts of amazing adventures.

Every guide comes from extensive exploration and research by our expert authors, all with a passion for their subjects. They are frequently praised, endorsed and used by clubs, instructors and outdoor organisations.

All our titles can now be bought as **e-books** and many as iPad and Kindle files and we will continue to make all our guides available for these and many other devices.

Our website shows any **new information** we've received since a book was published. Please do let us know if you find anything has changed, so that we can pass on the latest details. On our **website** you'll also find some great ideas and lots of information, including sample chapters, contents lists, reviews, articles and a photo gallery.

It's easy to keep in touch with what's going on at Cicerone, by getting our monthly **free e-newsletter**, which is full of offers, competitions, up-to-date information and topical articles. You can subscribe on our home page and also follow us on **Facebook** and **Twitter**, as well as our **blog**.

Cicerone – the very best guides for exploring the world.

CICERONE

2 Police Square Milnthorpe Cumbria LA7 7PY
Tel: 015395 62069 info@cicerone.co.uk
www.cicerone.co.uk